An Essay on Culture

An Essay on Culture

Symbolic Structure and Social Structure

Bennett M. Berger

UNIVERSITY OF CALIFORNIA PRESS

Berkeley / Los Angeles / London

University of California Press
Berkeley and Los Angeles, California

University of California Press, Ltd.
London, England

© 1995 by
The Regents of the University of California

Berger, Bennett M.
    An essay on culture : symbolic structure and social
structure / Bennett M. Berger.
      p. cm.
    Includes bibliographical references and index.
    ISBN 0-520-20016-0 (alk. paper).—ISBN 0-520-
20017-9 (pbk. : alk. paper)
    1. Culture. 2. Social structure. I. Title.
HM101.B4717 1995
306—dc20   94-33086
                                        CIP

Printed in the United States of America
9 8 7 6 5 4 3 2 1

The paper used in this publication meets the minimum re-
quirements of American National Standard for Information
Sciences—Permanence of Paper for Printed Library Materials, ANSI Z39.48–1984.

This one is for Kenneth and Stephanie,
my second generation of children who,
like their older siblings,
may read it some day.

CONTENTS

PREFACE

Having originated about ten years ago, this small book can hardly be considered hurried or topical—though there are several topical references in it. It began as an expensive proposal to establish a center for the study of culture at the University of California in San Diego. I sent it to the Ford Foundation, which was interested enough to ask me to come to New York and chat about it. I was so innocent of grantsmanship (having only once been involved as a principal investigator in a major research grant) that even as a senior professor I was unaware that one did not make formal "application" to Ford. If they liked what you had to say they asked you to come and chat further about it, which I did. Ford asked for more detail, which I provided, and one of Ford's representatives came to San Diego to talk with campus officials about their willingness to support the proposal. It apparently died right there. In a naive mistake for a senior professor to make, I had neglected even to try to garner the requisite political support from campus administrators for so ambitious a proposal, assuming its intellectual merits would be sufficient, and it fell as a casualty to that naiveté.

I can't exactly say that I am more sophisticated now, only a bit older. Unlike a lot of younger scholars, I sort of drifted into academic life without much thought about managing a career. As a graduate student,

I liked going to school, was good at it, and figured that I should (if I could) stay with what I liked and was good at. The only way to do that was to transform myself from a student to a professor, which I did, and did at a time when it was easy to do so and opportunities were abundant. It was a good career choice, spent doing mostly what I liked, teaching what I wanted, and writing only when the spirit moved me. Perhaps the greatest single blessing of academic life is never having to contend with a boss—which is as close as an employee in a modern bureaucracy can reasonably aspire to autonomy.

Although the proposal has never seen print, parts of this long essay have seen oral or print publication: some of it appeared as an article in *Theory and Society* (1991), a portion was published in French in *Sociologie et Société* (1989), and some is from an essay on Pierre Bourdieu that appeared in the *American Journal of Sociology* in 1986; other pieces of it have been given as lectures on various occasions. But they are all together here for the first time, in much revised form.

Several of the ideas in this essay were born in a joint seminar I offered with Richard Madsen, China scholar, co-author of *Habits of the Heart* (1985), and as good and generous a colleague as one could hope for. I thank him for the opportunity for dialogue he provided and continues to provide. My thanks, too, to another valuable colleague, Michael Schudson, and to my colleague/wife Chandra Mukerji for their readings of manuscript and always sharp commentaries. That they disagree with me in some fundamental respects does not make them less dear to me. I also profited from critical readings by Howard Becker, Judith Blau, Roy D'Andrade, Joseph Gusfield, and Tracy Strong. Thanks also to some very good graduate students (Eleanor Hodges, Sharon Hays, Perry Deess, Elizabeth Convert) who taught me a few things, who learned what I had to teach them about culture, and who resisted my influence to the end. None of them is accountable, of course, for what I say here.

If there is something final-sounding about these prefatory remarks, it is probably an expression of my retirement in 1991 from the University of California's faculty. I like to say that I've had my last wife, my last child, my last promotion, and this could well be my last book. Given my own materialist perspective on cultural matters, I have been alert to see whether (and how) my change of position has affected my thinking about these matters. It would be fun to say that my freedom from academic constraints has liberated my voice. But it's not that easy. Thirty-five years as an academic generates hard-to-break habits. Like smoking, it's hard to quit—hard to quit leaning on "perhaps" and "suggest" and "on the other hand" and "in terms of." Still, I've tried, not always successfully, to speak in a common language, and I've eliminated footnotes (though not a bibliography) because, as my title indicates, I intend this as an essay, not as a work of scholarship. I want to persuade you of the merits of looking at culture as I do. If I inform you in the process, that's gravy.

I

Sociology and Culture

INTRODUCTION

In spite of the Herculean efforts of scholars to agree on its meaning, "culture" remains one of those words that have eluded consensual usage. Like many highly abstract words, it is the common property of a variety of users who employ it to different purposes. Sociologists, anthropologists, and humanist scholars use it in somewhat different ways, and among educated people more generally, "culture" is likely to refer to those prestigious genres that confer on people familiar with them the designation "cultured."

Sociologists interested in the study of culture carry an ambivalent intellectual burden. As social *scientists* we try to discover, describe, understand, and explain the facts of social life as outcomes of major categorical forces that affect whom we come into contact with and how we come into contact with them—forces to which we are historically subject by virtue of our social placement (age, sex, race, ethnicity, income, occupation, etc.) and with which—and in which—most of us are more or less stuck. The "etc." is important because it implies an indefinitely large number of other potentially influential variables (ranging from family and education to birth order and physical appearance) that, in interaction with the other categorical forces, may create extremely complex patterns of events difficult even to describe in a specific case, much less understand or explain by reference to general principles.

On the other hand, the meaning of the very work we do as *social* scientists is itself a piece of culture, and we are not immune to the constraints and incentives of those categorical forces that, in affecting everyone, affect us too. Our professional education teaches us to be sensitive to and take account of those forces, and our technical training may even provide conceptual means and statistical techniques for neutralizing or controlling the influence of forces that, regardless of whether we are aware of them, tend to sustain or to undermine, in simple or complex ways, the culture in which we, like everyone else, are involved. The control, however, is seldom complete, seldom even fully deliberate or conscious; consequences, for example, are seldom fully anticipated. There is an ultimate sense in which we know not—at least not completely—what we do.

Still, "scientific" understanding is usually determinate understanding; events are understood when they are explained as necessary or more-or-less probable outcomes of the interaction of forces affecting the events. The more complete the determinism, the more complete the understanding. Human actors are seen as just that: "actors," or instruments of a script written by usually nameless others, past, present, or future. In our own locutions "history teaches," "society says," "posterity demands." Actors, of course, may sometimes improvise, alter the text, or bring startling interpretive originality to the script. But even when they do, the improvisation, the alteration, and the interpretation are usually (sometimes retrospectively) recognizable as such (rather than as cacophony, distortion, or derangement) and may eventually become part of a tradition or customary practice that "history teaches."

This determinist mode of understanding is, not surprisingly, often regarded as offensive in a culture where freedom, choice, and creativity are celebrated daily. The progress of understanding in social science is sometimes regarded as threatening to cherished ideas about freedom, and that constitutes the peculiar ambivalence of sociologists (and other citizens) who want more empirical knowledge of social life but want it without endangering sacred religious precepts or the quasi-sacred pieces of culture they hold dear.

Sometimes, when the knowledge acquired by social research is not controversial or volatile, the ambivalence is not very troubling. Social scientists can report facts, analyze correlations and causes, and reach conclusions without much concern for whether we (or anyone else) approve or disapprove them. Thus that we vote our economic interests (if we know them) more often than we vote against them, or that youth constitutes most of the market for pop music, or that we more often than not marry within ethnicity, religion, age-group, class, and residential locale are findings that agitate few people and that motivate few social scientists to take the trouble to quarrel with or attempt to rebut.

But when research does involve questions that touch deeply felt, unconscious culture or controversial ideologies (in these times, say, abortion, gender, ethnicity) two important consequences should be expected. First, the research conclusions are not likely to go unchallenged or unrebutted, particularly when they seem to threaten the conventional wisdoms of taken-for-granted culture; too many diverse interests may be at stake to allow that. Moreover, nearly every piece of social research is potentially vulnerable to criticism from one or another set of criteria shared by some professional groups, should they be motivated to invoke those criteria. The greater the extent to which research conclusions touch sensitive issues of culture or ideology, the greater the extent to which they are likely to undergo critical scrutiny from perhaps hostilely motivated others.

Second, researchers are usually at least partly aware of that prospect and often try to anticipate as much criticism as they can and respond to it before it is made. Hence the frequent presence of what I call "ideological work" in even very good cases of careful research. To the extent that researchers are aware of the cultural relevance of their findings and to the extent that they respond anticipatorily to imagined critics, the work is likely to contain a kind of *apologia pro vita sua*, sometimes implicit, sometimes out front. A substantial portion of part 2 of this book is devoted to the analysis of ideological work in nine exemplary pieces of empirical research on cultural themes.

Determinist modes of explanation are usually reductive, and in some academic milieux "reductionism" has become a nearly thoughtless pejorative when it is used in cultural explanation, particularly when efforts are made to explain felt culture (moral outrage, aesthetic revulsion, parental tenderness, i.e., *patterned* emotions) in terms of the conditions of social structure in which it is felt. In such instances explanation is often regarded as tantamount to "explaining away" as illusions things that are precious, like the sense of autonomy when we make choices or that moral catchall, the sense of "responsibility." For if our choices and behavior are "determined" can we be called to moral account for them? Moreover, if our autonomies are illusory doesn't that erode the grounds for resisting tyrannies or statist repression, which, in this view, will only be replaced by other forms of social control?

These questions, I think, are red herrings. In all but the hardest cases, statutes define responsibility adequately enough, and there are reasonably clear differences between official terror and choices made from a sense of internalized obligation or right. Even the choices we feel we want to make are drawn from the limited range of options affecting that feeling. Go over your own moment-to-moment and day-to-day choices and check it out. Some of us enjoy a greater range of options than others (although some may feel that too great a range can paralyze choice; think of waiting at the counter of Baskin-Robbins), and some struggle to increase their range of choice, sometimes against those trying to diminish it. It's usually those major categorical forces mentioned above that define the range at any given moment. But in addition, the choices from that range are usually affected by still other (perhaps more subtle, or "micro") categorical forces that determine choice, and it's largely ignorance of those and of the ways they interact that account for our apparently modest abilities to predict.

Still, most of our lives are reasonably predictable. It's what we call social order; most of the time we not only find this predictability untroubling but positively comforting, and when this predictable order is even mildly disrupted we sometimes call the disrupters "irresponsible." Where are choices most unpredictable? Probably at the most macro and micro ends of the continuum of interaction: the foreign and domestic policies of nations and the most intimate relations among lovers. With nations the categorical forces are most complex and the collective stakes highest, and so interests and consequences are most difficult to calculate. With intimates, prediction is difficult in part because interests and categorical forces are regarded as illegitimate (though they are of course present); in understanding intimate relations we usually resort to psychological rather than sociological analysis. Indeed, because psychological analysis often focuses on choices, far more psychology than sociology has filtered into the popular culture. American culture is full of "pop" (or vulgarized) psychology, but relatively little technical sociological thinking has been filtered into popular modes of thought.

But why on earth would anyone apparently want (as I do here) to make an argument promoting skepticism about freedom? The answer is complex. First, the quasi-sacred status of freedom discourages the efforts of all of us to become aware of the abstract categorical forces driving us and affecting our choices. Psychoanalysts know more than a little about how patients "resist" such awareness. Second, the celebration of freedom obstructs the explanatory efforts of social scientists by seeing these as efforts to "explain away" as illusory our precious sense of autonomy—although it's worth noting that we are usually more than willing to acknowledge determinisms when impugning the choices of others ("you're only saying [or doing] that because . . .") or when apologizing for our own choices made reluctantly. Third, in this determinist context, "freedom" becomes virtually the equivalent of ignorance, mystery, even mystification. Freedom becomes something we don't *want* to understand, or else we throw up our hands in despair of determinate understanding and call it freedom; in either case—irrational, obsessive, or demonic if we deplore it in the specific instance, and glorious, courageous, or heroic if we admire it—freedom is looked upon with more than a little awe.

For me, the great excitement of a sociology of culture lies in the challenge it represents to our understanding of freedom. In D. H. Lawrence's late novel of Australia, *Kangaroo*, he characterized his main protagonist as a man who traveled the world "looking for things not to give in to." A determinist sociology of culture, similarly, constitutes a continual testing of just how autonomous our choices are; of just how frequently we do or do not "give in" to the incentives, the intimidations, the temptations, the *pressures* that the social structure of our lives renders the flesh and the spirit heir to. Seen this way, a sociology of culture honors the mystery of freedom by taking it seriously enough to ask of those who cherish it just how much of it is actually or potentially present in their lives, and how often they prefer it to, say, prudence or duty, and under what conditions.

It is ironic that partisans of "agency," reacting against functionalist preoccupation with the study of conditions and consequences (and its neglect of individual motives), should be hostile to, for example, "conspiracy theories," which, whatever else they do, try to impute motives (i.e., "agency") to specific persons. It is also ironic that determinism should be perceived as a threat to freedom when in fact it must always struggle with its imperfect knowledge of the variables that affect choice. That ignorance may be just what permits actors to feel free, and the celebration of that feeling is at the root of our ambivalence about knowing more. There's plenty of evidence of hostility toward scientific modes of knowing when the knowledge could conceivably threaten something sacred. Thus, a sociology of culture becomes an adventure in ideas on quite uncertain terrain.

Short books don't warrant long introductions, so I'll end briefly. I understand culture not as something transcendent, sacred, or otherwise ethereal (although certainly, sometimes, mysterious), but as a set of tools, or in Ann Swidler's language, a set of strategies constituting a repertoire—instruments, like hammers, wristwatches, and bureaucratic memos that get us through our days and help us make it through the night. This usage is not unfamiliar to anthropologists who have long regarded baskets, pots, and arrowheads as pieces of "material culture." But sociologists and humanist scholars have often balked at extending this usage to "ideal" or symbolic culture, to the meanings we carry in our heads and (culturally speaking) our "hearts."

I want not to balk. I want to assert, argue, persuade that such symbols/meanings, like baskets, pots, and watches, are about getting us through the days and nights we are more or less stuck with, and in doing so providing us with a sense of having got through with some dignity—dignity itself, of course, being a precious piece of culture. I do not believe that to see the matter this way is to demean (de-mean) the dignity; it is only to look it hard in the face, ask it tough questions, and hope it will not give in.

Culture is so sensitive an area of study because it is a surrogate for religion, for what is self-evidently good, true, or otherwise worthy. Not all of the facts of social life are "cultural," but some are—meanings, many of which inhabit a quasi-sacred realm, revealed and conveyed by custom, utterance, and other symbolic evocations. Hence to treat them routinely, as one would any other set of social facts, with an eye to pattern, recurrence, correlation, and cause, inviting reductive explanation, is to skirt sacrilege. Yet culture invites reductionism, as my colleague Tracy Strong reminded me, *by virtue of its symbolic nature;* it is we who make and unmake symbols, and a sociology of culture is the study of how we do it.

We Americans don't any more, like the late Ayatollah Khomeini, condemn alleged blasphemers to death (and offer enormous rewards to the killer), but not long ago we used to lynch black men and boys for what were considered improper remarks or gestures toward white ladies. I'm grateful that I incur no such risk in writing about culture in a resolutely secular way. I would like to believe that were the risk greater I would still write as I do here. But I can't be sure of that, and I am grateful too that my freedom will not be so tested.

1 / VOCABULARIES OF ANALYSIS

If what follows seems in places oatmealy or otherwise muddy and banal, blame it on the middling level of abstraction I'm reaching for. I will not attempt to deal with the highest levels of cultural abstraction, like Modernism, Postmodernism, the Renaissance, the Enlightenment, or Judeo-Christian Civilization, but rather with what I call pieces or chunks of culture, like norms of marriage, courtship and divorce, linguistic usage, taken-for-granted categories of thought, mass media images, varieties of taste, and age-grading practices.

Still, my treatment will be abstract enough for many tastes and too abstract for some. An absence of prose vividness is the price one pays for abstraction. Like everything I write, I always (and unrealistically) hope it will be of interest not only to sociologists and anthropologists (and perhaps other academics) but also to that disappearing constituency that publishers hopefully characterize as the educated general reader. So although I will try to exemplify with concrete—even provocative—illustrations whenever I can, I'm actually trying to say something fairly *general* about the concept of culture and its relations to ideology, politics, and social structure. Much of it is necessarily not original, and the level of generality requires some sacrifice in concreteness and detail. Moreover I'm trying to say it without revealing—or indulging—much of my own tastes and preferences in culture, politics, and ideology (although attentive readers will no doubt detect some of them), and the strain of such reticence probably shows.

The social sciences and humanities recurrently generate new theoretical vocabularies (structuralism, functionalism, deconstruction, semiotics, symbolic interactionism, ethnomethodology, postmodernism, etc.) to apply to old problems that, ever recalcitrant, almost predictably defeat the efforts of old theoretical vocabularies to solve them. There remains, of course, more than a little ambiguity about what, exactly, is "solved" by new theoretical understandings of, say, racism (a piece of culture) or problems of age-grading in adolescence or colonialism or the mysteries of a classic literary text. Understanding does not always provide solutions to the problems it indicates; knowledge, *pace* Foucault, is not always power. (Irony, for example, is a prominent feature of discourse in the humanities and social sciences, and what it often conveys is knowledge *without* the power to act on it.) Indeed, much of academic life outside the hard sciences (and even occasionally within those citadels) consists, it seems to me, in the invention of new languages for the analysis of ever-knotty issues.

But the new languages do not always designate new ideas. The language of "practices," for example, is very much evident in contemporary cultural analysis. Clifford Geertz is sometimes credited with having helped reorient cultural studies away from Talcott Parsons's focus on norms/values to an empirical focus on the specific cultural practice of a people. This may well be the case, but the "new" language of practices surely evokes one of the older conceptions of culture as the "customs" of a people. What else are the "mores" and "folkways" of W. G. Sumner if not practices? That vocabulary goes back to the turn of the century, if not earlier.

Even my own middle-range effort to focus on pieces or chunks of culture evokes the vocabulary of cultural "items," "traits," "patterns," and "configurations," a set of terms associated with the revered name of Alfred Kroeber, and that, in the 1950s, all students were required to learn when taking courses in cultural anthropology. Those terms, indicating an ascending order of abstraction, seem to have disappeared from the usage of current cultural studies without, I should add, any devastating criticism that I know of which could be regarded as responsible for their disappearance. Similarly, the French sociologist Pierre Bourdieu's idea of "systematic misrecognition" (almost a biblical "they know not what they do") evokes the currently discredited idea of "false consciousness" (discredited largely owing to its association with hard Marxism), although Bourdieu uses the idea to suggest that misunderstanding is a systematic part of the process of maintaining and reproducing the social order of things; that is, we all have *interests* in misunderstanding or misrecognizing the meanings of the culture in which we are involved.

Poststructuralist language is a particularly egregious case of new vocabularies describing old ideas. The "social imaginary" seems to be a clumsier way of referring to what was once called "myth." "Discourse," thanks largely to Foucault and the linguists, has apparently replaced "discussion," and "narrative" often refers to what used to be called "common understandings." Still, for all its de rigueur jargon (which, of course, tells us that its audience is an academic one) poststructuralism, in its deconstructive "project" (another linguistic dead-giveaway) does help weaken the hegemony of language by sensitizing us to the ways in which taken-for-granted concepts govern our thinking and by reminding us of their historically constituted character (and hence of their vulnerability to deconstruction). In fact, original thinkers often become "major" thinkers by successfully altering the vocabularies in which old problems are discussed; they create a "discourse," often by "dissing" the present course of discussion.

Nevertheless, there is still an image in my mind of persistent old problems, bent—as if with life of their own—on preserving themselves unsolved, rampantly triumphant over old theories and vocabularies, and eager to meet and defeat the onslaught of the new. That image, however reified, suggests the wisdom of prudence, a certain diffidence in the claims one makes. What is offered here is not a new theory, but a reasonably systematic effort to organize and deploy old ideas (and perhaps a few new ones) in familiar vocabularies for combat against old problems, in hope of winning a few skirmishes in the long war of conscious understanding. The conflict metaphors are deliberate; cultural understanding requires attention not only to image, sound, word, gesture, and the symbolic character of human things but (as Weber put it) to the material as well as the ideal interests of persons and groups in those symbolic realms. The point is that such efforts are seldom unopposed.

Conscious cultural understanding is opposed precisely because the material and ideal interests of some persons and groups are ill-served by such understanding, and the kinds of disservice done may range from the micro-personal to the macro-collective. There are, of course, many things we don't understand in any genuinely reliable sense but that we need to believe we understand in order to cope with the unavoidable tasks of everyday life. Among the scores of examples, my favorite is the task of raising children, which most of us must do at one or another time in circumstances where relatively little is reliably known about the relation of child-rearing practices to developmental outcomes. Still, many parents will assert great confidence in the wisdom of their particular expert authority on children, revealing thereby only that there is something close to a consensus among Americans that requires expertise (usually "scientific" but sometimes biblical or otherwise "traditional") to sanction or defend one's childrearing practices even in the absence of truly conclusive evidence.

But in addition to the many things we need to think we understand in circumstances where knowledge is insufficient to sustain real understanding but where facing the fact that we are groping in the dark appears intolerable, there are many other things that we don't want to understand rationally, and these are by no means limited to the kinds of problems psychiatrists typically deal with. Psychoanalytic therapists generally encounter people (patients) whose repression or other lack of conscious understanding has generated the problems bringing the patient to the therapeutic couch. But there are many other kinds of more or less willed ignorance that appear perfectly normal; the ignorance does no disservice to the person's interests whereas conscious understanding might well do them damage. A person with a thoughtlessly beautiful and fluid tennis serve may have little interest in risking its becoming awkward and ill-coordinated by self-conscious efforts to show a casual admirer exactly how he or she does it; if one is a "natural," becoming unnatural (i.e., consciously and analytically deliberate) is something to be avoided. In modern societies romantic love is *properly* mystified, and efforts to understand or analyze it rationally are disdainfully regarded by many as ludicrous, woodenheaded, or worse. One is, after all, supposed to "fall" in love, not rationally choose it. Parents with interests in being "good" mothers and fathers (or at least not bad ones) must think that they know the difference; hence they have interests in not recognizing the inconclusive character of the evidence regarding permissiveness, discipline, "tough love," or any of the other available guides to parenting. Resistance by traditional academics to the establishment of popular culture and "multicultural" studies in university curricula was in part a response to the sensed threat the study of folk, ethnic, tribal, peasant, or third-world culture represented to the presumable superiority of Western high culture, by revealing the class and national character of cultural domination. In all four cases material and ideal interests are at risk.

2 / CULTURE: VARIETIES OF USAGE

"Culture" is one of the most common words in current usage by the social sciences and the humanities. It is also increasingly familiar in ordinary usage beyond the narrow confines of academic disciplines. Like many, if not most, abstract words in common usage there has never been much consensus apparent—or necessary—among users on its precise meaning, which is one reason why serious scholars are constrained to define their usage carefully when invoking such words. In fact, efforts to be precise in ordinary language-use risk bringing routine social interaction to a sudden halt. Harold Garfinkel has shown in some of his well-known "experiments" how breaching some of the tacit rules of politeness that constrain us *not* to ask for clarification of vague words in ordinary conversation can create anxiety, then explosive anger, and perhaps a stricken anomie. Don't ask someone who utters an innocent "have a good day" what he or she means. Don't behave like a polite guest in your family's home unless you want to drive your mother up the wall. Trying to learn a foreign language as an adult can be a depressing experience early in the process when one realizes that one understands perhaps half of what is being said in conversation. Some comfort may be provided by realizing that even in one's native language one can be uncertain about how much one understands—or can reasonably expect to understand—of what others say and write. Nevertheless, hope springs eternal, and the aim of the following pages is to articulate a clear concept of culture that embraces the varieties of the word's usage over the centuries; clear enough in any case to enable the concept to serve as the central focus for sociological studies of the phenomena from which the concept is abstracted.

Raymond Williams (1976) tells us that, from its earliest usage, the word has always designated the cultivation or tending of something—as for example in agri-culture. In the sixteenth century and after, the tending was gradually extended in elite usage to include the cultivation of prestigious human qualities: mind, manners, spirit, sensibility, "taste." By the eighteenth century, elite Europeans used the word ethnocentrically, to distinguish between the highly refined civil cultivation achieved by privileged western Europeans (and therefore by their "civilization") and what was perceived as the comparatively primitive development of such human qualities both in non-Europeans (Elias 1983) and in the second of Disraeli's "two nations" (i.e., the poor). Note, however, another distinction made in some old sociological textbooks (e.g., MacIver 1937) between civilization (the kind of cultivation occurring in technologically advanced societies with a highly differentiated class system) and culture (the kind of cultivation developed in traditional homogeneous societies). That distinction, although currently moribund, could become increasingly important with the spread of cultural pluralism.

It was partly in reaction against the ethnocentric usage by European elites that, toward the end of the eighteenth century, the German historian Herder introduced perhaps the first usage of "culture" as a substantive (or reified) noun, suggesting that all peoples "had" *a* culture. It took another hundred years, however, for that wholistic usage of "culture" (as a people's "way of life") to become established as the standard basic concept of cultural anthropology through Edward Tylor's influential usage in his *Primitive Culture* (1958), and that usage has generated many major and minor variations (Kroeber and Kluckhohn 1952).

Of course, to speak of peoples as "having" a culture implies a relation of possession, and possession itself conveys the double meaning of possessing and being possessed by (or having and "being had"). To have or to possess a culture, then, is in some respects necessarily to be had or to be possessed by it. Notice how the English "have to" conveys both possession and necessity. People sometimes called "sociopaths" may be described as those who have been dispossessed of an important part (the constraining part) of their culture—or who never "had" it. One might even reasonably assert that it is more accurate to say that culture "has" us than that we have it. Notice how knowledge of other cultures often weakens the grip of our own culture on us—perhaps one of the origins of the familiar distinction between cosmopolitans and provincials. There is an irreducible sense in which culture is something that, once we have subjectively internalized it and made it "ours," we are objectively stuck with—at least for some time, perhaps until changed circumstances create conditions that make potentially alternative cultures accessible.

As twentieth-century anthropologists pursued their analyses of tribal ways of life it became conventional to distinguish between "material culture" (tools, artifacts, things, *objets*) and "nonmaterial" (or "ideal") culture (meanings, symbols, values), the latter being imputed to or inferred from material objects, practices involving their use, and other customary behavior—including, of course, the use of language itself. Anthropologists and sociologists sometimes used the phrase "ideal culture" in a different sense: to distinguish between (1) behavior that the culture "ideally" prescribed and (2) how "real" behavior was actually distributed among a population. To use an interpersonal (micro) example: a middle-class father might tell his fourteen-year-old daughter about to go out on a first date to be home by 11 P.M. (ideal rule: nice girls should be home by that hour.) Arriving home at 1 A.M., she might explain to her angry father that "all the girls stay out that late"—the actual distribution, maybe somewhat exaggerated. A trivial example, perhaps. But virtually the same issue, at an institutional (macro) level, was at stake when, in the autumn of 1991, Senator Alan Cranston of California was formally reprimanded by the Ethics Committee of the U.S. Senate for his dealings with Charles Keating and the now-defunct Lincoln Savings and Loan Association. Senator Cranston, it seems, had broken no laws nor even any of the formal rules of the U.S. Senate, but he had done some major favors for Mr. Keating, a wealthy and influential contributor to his campaigns. In a speech responding to the Ethics Committee's reprimand, Senator Cranston revealed no remorse and, indeed, suggested that most of his Senate colleagues were guilty of showing favoritism to important and influential constituents (versus the democratic "ideal norm" of treating constituents with equal respect and deference). In Cranston's case, of course, his ill-advised favoritism cost the taxpayers approximately two billion dollars (reason enough, perhaps, for reprimand), but whether his ethics were more reprehensible than most of his unreprimanded colleagues is an open question—less open, of course, if the outrage to ideal interests is measured by its material costs, as is not infrequently the case.

Sociologists were generally less interested than anthropologists in the study of material culture as such. They customarily limited their usage of the word "culture" to what anthropologists called nonmaterial culture—particularly to "norms," which, in the influential usage of Parsons and other functionalists, were conceived as a relatively specific form of (the more abstract) values, metaphorically "written" into the scripts of social roles, prescribing appropriate or expected behavior (and proscribing other behavior) in particular kinds of recurrent situations.

The long-current "humanistic" usage of the word "culture" dates from Tylor's contemporary Matthew Arnold, whose influential *Culture and Anarchy* [1869] (1971) defined the word as the *best* that has been thought and said. It is from Arnold and from the ethnocentric usage of eighteenth-century elites that the still most widespread popular usage of the word (for example when we describe someone as "cultured") derives. A cultured person in this sense is one in *possession* of the best that has been thought and said ("the finer things in life"), and those possessions were typically acquired through established forms or genres in which the "best" people were typically trained and educated: language, literature, the arts, fashion and comportment, religion, philosophy, history, and (more recently) science.

Of course, to speak of culture as "possessed" suggests that those who possess it own it, both in the sense of actual property they may properly use, and in the sense of culture as "a property of" human beings. The two senses are obviously related, and have enabled some scholars to see the differential possession of culture as property deployable as a kind of capital to be invested or otherwise used to one's own advantage—even "violently," as in Bourdieu's idea of "symbolic violence," in which some persons are morally intimidated or otherwise made to feel inferior owing to their lack of, or ignorance of, specific forms of cultural capital.

Cultured persons (in the Western sense), then, are those highly cultivated in elite forms; competent in showing the kinds of knowing that command the highest prestige (Jaeger and Selznick 1964; Johnson 1979)—if not necessarily personal esteem. Elite cultivation could be, and sometimes was, excessive or arrogant and could generate resentment against some persons instead of respect, particularly as egalitarianism spread in Europe and the United States; thus we have foppery and snobbery as vices, learnedness as pedantry, and caricatures of the extended little finger alongside the raised teacup. Egalitarianism was stronger in the U.S. than in Europe, and elite cultivation was more intimidating in Europe than in the U.S. to those excluded from it. Indeed, in "pioneer" countries colonized by the British (the U.S., South Africa, Australia, New Zealand), elite cultivation was often subtly disdained as feminine, whereas the more "manly" virtues were identified with the vigorous tasks of taming the wilderness and building a civilization in the virgin country: mechanics, carpentry, agriculture, entrepreneurship, logging, animal husbandry, and so on. "Culture" was left to women— and feminized men (Ann Douglas 1977). Bourdieu's recurrent use of the phrase "legitimate culture" (where Americans would use the phrase "high culture" or "elite culture") implies an assumed imputation of illegitimacy to "popular culture," something far less likely to be taken for granted in an American context. The very distinction between high and popular culture, in fact, had to be deliberately created among Americans (Levine 1988; DiMaggio 1986a). In its middle-class versions in the U.S.

such prestige as was attached to high culture became, in Santayana's phrase (notice, again, the element of disdain), "the genteel tradition."

In anthropology, sociology, and the humanities, then, we find three distinct but related usages, and these usages can be arranged in an order going from the general to the specific. Anthropology's usage is most general, including, as it does, practices (customs), objects, and ideas (i.e., the abstract meanings practices and objects convey). Indeed, for most anthropologists culture is an all-encompassing concept, roughly analogous to social structure or social organization for sociologists, or the market for most economists (Boltanski and Thevenot 1991).

Sociology's standard usage of culture is more specific than anthropology's, including only abstract ideas (norms, values, style, strategies, repertoires, etc.) and the symbols that imply or represent them. In the humanities the usage has been still more specific, limiting it to the best or noblest ideas as they are formally expressed in the most prestigious established genres. It is only in recent decades that literary and historical scholars have begun to include the materials of "popular," ethnic, or mass culture (film, TV, pop music, etc.) as topics of research and as features of university curricula—sometimes as part of a deliberate effort to democratize culture studies and to oppose the hegemony of "high culture." Were it not for that hegemony, the very phrase "popular culture" would be more widely recognized as the redundancy it is; without at least *some* currency (i.e., popularity) culture would become idiosyncrasy or a curiosity.

Many of the recent debates over multiculturalism and the "canon" in American universities are obviously rooted in the difference between the social science usage of culture (normative ways of life) and the humanist usage of culture (the best ideas expressed in the most prestigious established forms). Without getting into that highly politicized debate here, I think it is clear that the "conservative" partisans in this controversy adopt a conception of culture as the best of the heritage of Western Civilization, whereas the "radicals" adopt a conception of culture as the lived lives of ordinary people, which should be dignified (if not actually celebrated) by study and analysis—one more example of the now-overt, now-hidden tensions between humanistic and scientific modes of understanding.

To use the neo-Kantian distinction, students of culture are usually interested in *noumena*, inferred from objectively observable (and in principle measurable) *phenomena*. Even the interest of anthropologists in artifacts is primarily for the information about meanings they reveal. Not all students of culture, however, adopted the radically nonpositivist posture conveyed in the distinction between *Geisteswissenschaften* (cultural or spiritual sciences) and *Naturwissenschaften* (natural sciences), for that distinction implied radically different cognitive aims and methods of research. Whereas natural sciences aimed at "explaining" the phenomena they scrutinized by experimental or quasi-experimental research designs (comparative studies, statistical controls on variables) to reveal nature's regularities, the social and cultural sciences aimed at "understanding" (*verstehen*) the phenomena they scrutinized through fundamentally imaginative or projective efforts of intuition and interpretation, which connected the newer social sciences to the older humanities (history, philosophy, belles lettres). Weber's emphasis on subjective meaning stems from this German distinction, in contrast, for example, to Durkheim's more positivist conception of "social facts." Theoretical controversy continues to this day over the merits and relevance of positivist and interpretive (or scientific and humanistic, or naturalist/ "realist" and edifying) modes of comprehending culture (Geertz 1973; Mary Douglas 1986; Spiro 1987; Clifford and Marcus 1986; Swidler 1986; Schudson 1989; Schneider 1993; Thompson, Ellis, and Wildavsky 1990), and over the possibilities of combining them. These controversies aside for the moment, the central focus of cultural studies is the interpretive reading of meanings from the discourse and other behavior of persons and groups. These are studied either ethnographically or historically through observed social practices or through the texts and other objects produced by, and surviving, these social practices; or through some combination of these data.

3 / CULTURAL STUDIES

Given the traditional focus of anthropologists on relatively homogeneous tribal societies, their studies of culture typically use (in addition to artifacts) such formal materials as myth, ritual, song, legend, folktale, and ceremony (usually conceived as representative of the whole society) in describing and analyzing the important symbols, values, and meanings that are affirmed and conveyed by them, usually through recurrent institutional practice. The ethnographic literature is full of field studies that may be so characterized. The so-called new anthropology has increasingly emphasized the interpretive dimensions of ethnographic studies, including self-reflexive preoccupations by the ethnographer. This emphasis has been influenced by perceived discrepancies between the stated aims of the research and the actual behavior of the researcher, or between the fieldwork itself and the final rendering of it in an ethnographic report. The ethnographer, formerly either invisible or a neutral instrument recording the life of a people, moves front and center, *eliciting* findings and sentiently involved in them. The ethnography itself (i.e., the text), formerly preoccupied with documenting findings and supporting epistemological claims, becomes either a problem of authorship (in Geertz's terms "an honest story honestly told") or a meditation on the ethnographer's relation to the people studied. These considerations have moved ethnographers away from the positivist, and toward the humanist, "interpretive" paradigm.

A model of description and interpretation somewhere between these poles is contained in the well-known essay on the Balinese cockfight by Clifford Geertz. The point in such work is to "read" such artifacts or events for meanings, for what they reveal about the culture of a people. That's the interpretive part. The positivist part is to ask why *these* meanings rather than those, why expressed this way rather than that, and to seek answers in their relations with other dimensions of social structure and culture, in this case, for example, by comparisons with cockfighting in other times and places.

Geertz's account, of course, is dazzling; a virtuoso interpretive performance comparable, say, to Edmund Wilson's use of the wound-and-the-bow metaphor in his reading of the myth of Philoctetes, or Vladimir Nabokov's lectures on Dickens and Jane Austen. The comparison to novelists and literary critics is not inadvertent. They are not often asked how they know what they claim to know; indeed, novelists tend to be especially elusive about their "claims." "Never trust the teller, trust the tale," said D. H. Lawrence, relying as he did on the persuasiveness of the "data" in the story itself, rather than on commentaries (authorial or critical) about it. The persuasiveness of novelists and critics rests not on a restricted conception of evidence systematically marshaled to test the validity of an assertion, but on the subtlety and originality of their insights, the coherence of their conceptions, the aesthetic force conveyed by a prose style. Geertz's account is predominantly *Geisteswissenschaft*; there is no answer in the text of "Notes on the Balinese Cockfight" to the mundane *Naturwissenschaft* question: where's the evidence to support Geertz's assertion that the social status of a Balinese is unaffected by the cockfight, despite the enormous sums wagered on its outcome? I don't doubt for a moment that Balinese, particularly bird owners and those who bet on the fights, identify themselves with their cocks. But it never seems to have occurred to Geertz to ask whether Balinese who fight or bet on cocks identify *more* than those who don't, or whether Balinese cockfighting is different from cockfighting in other places. I'm not surprised that he didn't ask those questions; they're not as, well, "interesting" as the questions he does ask. But an answer would have provided a kind of test for several of the meanings he does read into the sport.

The most familiar kinds of studies of culture by humanists are histories (of art, ideas, philosophy, theology, and, more recently, "social" history) and critical interpretations of texts, images, and performances, usually in the elite arts (though, as I have suggested, increasingly in the popular arts), thus exemplifying Matthew Arnold's conception of culture as the best that has been thought and said. But over the past two or three decades something odd has happened in the relationship of humanists and social scientists to cultural studies. Interpretive social science has been heavily "theoretical" for a long time. A theory explicitly told students of empirical materials how to conceptualize them, what aspects of them were important to scrutinize, and how ("methodology") to look at them rigorously. It also provided social scientists with an armory of technical concepts (easily caricaturable by historians and belletrists) to interpret or explain the meanings of the data. Until well into the 1960s sociologists were consistently satirized or otherwise caricatured by poets, literary critics, and historians for the impenetrable jargon of their concepts, for the woodenness of their prose, for the banality of their conclusions (Berger 1971). On the other hand, until the invasion of French structuralism, American literary criticism, despite René Wellek, had traveled its routes largely without serious and comprehensive theoretical baggage (Freudians and Marxists, minority tendencies, were notable exceptions); the critic confronted a classic literary text armed only, or primarily, with a finely tuned aesthetic sensibility; T. S. Eliot, describing Henry James as a "mind too fine to be violated by ideas," recommended only intelligence as the critic's basic equipment. Now things are far less clear. Geertz speaks of the blurring of scholarly genres (a properly effective and self-serving defense of the blurring of genres in his own later work), and he reads the Balinese cockfight not unlike a literary critic might read a classic text—with an intelligent eye, that is, rather than a visibly explicit commitment to a theory.

But literary humanists accord increasing prestige to their theorists of interpretation (semioticians, structuralists, and their successors), who treat texts not unlike theory-laden social scientists treated social behavior—deploying an armory of explicit concepts and techniques designed to induce the text to yield up some of the lasting mysteries of culture:

recurrence, pattern, meaning, the power of symbols to move emotions. These days it is as easy to find satiric and disdainful caricatures of impenetrable poststructuralisms as it was thirty-five years ago to find such characterizations of sociologists. It was almost as if the social sciences had too much theory, the humanities not enough; by the 1960s, old-fashioned lit-crit, without explicit theory, was pretty much exhausted as a genre, and as the social sciences became increasingly empirical and quantitative, increasingly *Naturswissenschaft*, lit-crit became increasingly theoretical; "literary theory" became a big topic in the universities, borrowing much of its thinking from European sociologists, linguists, and social philosophers. Even many historians, traditionally scornful of overt theorizing, began to realize that their disdain was only a way of protecting the preconceptions with which they actually worked. Whether humanists and social scientists are passing each other going in opposite directions or moving toward a synthesis of scientific and humanistic modes of understanding remains to be seen.

Sociology came late to academic scholarship and inherited both the neoclassic/elite tradition and the romantic/democratic tradition. As Robert Nisbet (1953) has shown, many of the basic concepts of sociology (status, tradition, function, etc.) in Europe were developed from the conservative political ideas of European aristocrats attempting a counterrevolution against the events in France of 1789–1794. But as Robert Merton (Merton and Nisbet 1961) has pointed out, sociology's lateness on the academic scene in the U.S. obliged it to take as its initial subjects some of the humbler, leftover materials of human behavior (like persons, data have prestige—high, middle, low; the recent establishment of elevated subjects like science and medicine as subfields of sociological study has helped increase the prestige of sociology as a whole, in spite of the occasional tendencies in both subfields to adopt a demystifying, even debunking, posture toward the pieties of science and medicine). The choicer, more prestigious materials had earlier been picked off by political science (the state, government, international relations), economics (money, business, finance) and jurisprudence (law, justice). Anthropology had long been linked with the colonial policies of imperialist nations. The major institutional focus left to early sociology was the family, which since Roman times (when it was the habitus of women and slaves) was the place where nothing of much public (i.e., noble) significance occurred. Other typical materials for American sociology were crime and delinquency, children and the aged, immigrants and the poor, the lame, the addicted, the insane, and other wretched—all of which fed the American perfectionist appetite for ameliorating "social problems." The very materials of sociology, in short, were often contemptible, so much so that early American sociologists were discouraged from having any direct, first-hand research contact with them: the preference being for only indirect contact through those, like welfare workers, whose professional obligations required direct contact.

As the historian Sam Warner (1962) has pointed out, the conservative and aristocratic European heritage of sociology was balanced on this side of the Atlantic in the early years of the twentieth century by the ameliorative approaches of social work to the "less fortunate" (Jane Addams and the Settlement House movement), and by the early prominence of Protestant preachers of the liberal social gospel (and their sons) as teachers and students of sociology. Marxists—and Jews—did not appear in American sociology in any significant numbers until later. The liberal Protestant faith (supported for a while by the Rockefeller philanthropies, which had the same high Protestant outlook) was that research, producing greater knowledge of human society, would "confirm" liberal values. The "ideological bankruptcy" imputed to liberalism in recent years is an expression of the belief that that faith has not been confirmed. The truth was knottier than previously thought, and it did not seem to set one free.

4 / CULTURAL PLURALISM

One of the consequences of this sociological preoccupation with subordinate or disadvantaged groups is that the concept of culture became more differentiated. Where Herder and the anthropological tradition had reclaimed culture from elites by showing that all peoples had a culture (although some evolutionists continued to insist that some were higher than others), the sociological tradition made it evident that culture both was a property of "peoples" (in the sense of tribe, ethnic group, or nation) and was applicable to groups constituting something considerably less than a "whole" society. The basic insight here was that perhaps any group, sufficiently segregated or otherwise insulated in time and place to selectively interact—exclusively or primarily—with other members of that group, could be expected to generate distinctive "ways of life"—including a language, dialect, or argot, and an indigenous set of ideas and customs not shared by outsiders.

A sociological literature was subsequently born describing and analyzing the "cultures" of crime and delinquency, social classes, age groups, occupational groups, ethnic-immigrant groups, lately gender culture—even the culture of families. Family culture here refers not only to the practices made meaningful to all persons who live in families by virtue of their participation (or "membership") in that small social structure—intimate relations, gender division of labor, age-grading, modes of child rearing, kinship rights and obligations and the special loyalties and antagonisms generated by them; it also means that in some respects each family has a unique culture, meanings only *its* members share—private jokes, nicknames, presents opened on Christmas eve or Christmas morn, restricted codes (Bernstein 1975)—the meanings that come from intimacy over a long stretch of time and that nonmembers cannot be expected to understand. Sociology, in short, through its research involvements with groups smaller than whole societies, gave us the concept of "subculture," which took its place beside such related ideas as ambience, milieu, sense of place, walk of life, and so on (Merton 1957; Spitzer 1942).

Several of the subcultures associated with these smaller social structures were in some respects not only different from but marginal or offensive to the dominant culture of the nation, and sometimes, therefore, created problems of social control for the nation's central authorities. Some of these subcultures could be (and were) conceptualized by sociologists under the rubric "deviance," and over the years several theories about deviance were generated (Sutherland 1956; Merton 1957; Cohen 1955; Lemert 1967; Becker 1963; Katz 1988). One important feature of this intellectual development was the implicit (and increasingly explicit) *democratization* of the concept of culture it contained.

In earlier incarnations the study of what eventually was called "deviance" had been stigmatized by designating such phenomena with terms like "social disorganization" and "social pathology." "Deviance," though trailing a still somewhat unsavory aroma, smells rather sweeter than "social pathology." But this pluralizing process of conceptual evolution from disorganization to pathology to deviance may not yet be ended. Two important subsequent developments are worth noting: first, as the discovery and recognition of subcultures proliferated, it became increasingly difficult, especially in the U.S., to locate and concretely describe the main or dominant culture in terms of which the cultures of smaller, more isolated, more localized (in time or place) social groups were "sub." ("Middle America" was sometimes used in efforts to designate it.) This had very practical consequences, as major political parties had to devote increasingly calculated attention to latent cultural predispositions in strategically putting together majority coalitions in national electoral campaigns: for example, the "southern strategy" of the Republican Party that came to fruition in Richard Nixon's victories after the national Democratic Party's commitment to civil rights legislation alienated many traditionally Democratic southern voters. In this context, the conventional wisdom now is that the Democratic Party allowed itself to be captured by "minorities" and other "special interests" (subcultures), thus permitting the Republicans to dominate presidential elections for more than twenty years.

Second, although ethnic pride goes back a lot further than the Civil Rights movement of the 1960s, ethnic subcultures and their preservation became increasingly respectable during that period (the "Roots" phenomenon), competing with the formerly assumed idea of the "melt-ing pot." Other subcultures (gays, feminists, the handicapped) that had been designated "deviant" became increasingly contentious politically. Their social movements demanded from the increasingly elusive, some-times defensive dominant culture not merely toleration (which implies a patronizing posture by those who tolerate) but equal rights, equal sta-tus, equal honor to the meaningful practices that defined and dignified their cultural distinctiveness as groups.

There is a lot of conflict, of course, but also much ambiguity in American culture over issues like these. The movements, in the 1960s and after, affirming ethnic pride among blacks and latinos grew from disillusion with the promise of assimilation. Racism was so deeply em-bedded among white Americans, it was believed (on the Left of the Civil Rights movement), that the disappearance of prejudice against people of color could be imagined only in Martin Luther King's most visionary and eloquent rhetoric. The problem, of course, was that to say "I'm—-——and I'm proud" was a sort of violation of the American ethic that defined pride (when it wasn't simply hubris or sin) as legitimate only when it was attached to achievements rather than to attributes, like race or ethnicity, with which one was willy-nilly stuck from birth. Therefore when white people on the political Left affirmed the ethnic pride of "minorities," it almost inevitably contained a note of patronization or disingenuousness since such affirmation would not have been extended to WASPs or other white ethnics, among whom expressions of ethnic pride would be seen as chauvinism.

Moreover, an emphasis on ethnic identity is itself politically ambigu-ous. Since the 1960s it has had a mostly leftish political cast in the U.S., although earlier celebrations of ethnic identity by, say, Irish-American or Italian-American groups seldom had explicit political content and were primarily religious or "purely" cultural celebrations. In Europe, on the other hand, "ancient" ethnic identities are often invented and exploited by the political Right in the interests of xenophobia. Ethnicity may well be a cultural sword of sorts, but it is without question a double-edged one.

It is also important to note, in this respect, the increasingly standard (and significant) usage of the word "community," as in "black community," "gay community," "latino community," or "feminist community," where "blacks," "gays," "latinos," and "feminists" would seem to be adequate as terms of reference. "Community" in this sense functions to convey the notion that the persons so designated are not merely aggregates or collectivities or categories defined by a single criterion, but social groups possessing a common culture—a linguistic practice that disguises the differences or conflicts within each of these groups, and invites the inference (correct or not) that the imputed common culture produces an imputed collective identity.

Humanist scholars, too, noted this increasing differentiation of the concept of culture with respect to their own traditional materials. Historians devoted more attention to histories of the family, women, children, peasants, working classes, and other subordinate groups; to histories of the criminal and the insane and other relatively voiceless groups which, having left few or difficult-to-unearth documents, had not had their culture or historical experience adequately recorded (Thompson 1964; Gutman 1976; Ariès 1962; Hobsbawm 1964; Scull 1979; Foucault 1965; Ladurie 1974). Critics and historians of literature and art did something analogous concerning questions of aesthetics and taste in art, fashion, and related matters. Although debates over the merits of elite and popular cultural forms can be traced to the early eighteenth century (Lowenthal 1956), beginning in the 1920s (Van Wyck Brooks 1958) and continuing over several decades, there was increasing discussion of highbrow, middlebrow, and lowbrow tastes (Lynes 1957; MacDonald 1965; Fiedler 1971) and of mass culture, class cultures, and folk culture (Shils 1957; Eliot 1949; Hoggart 1967; Thompson 1964; Williams 1981; the Birmingham School—see Collins et al. 1986). By 1974 Herbert Gans had published his influential *Popular*

Culture and High Culture in which he argued that "taste cultures" (there were five major ones, he said, corresponding mostly to social classes) were equally worthy of public respect and support, and equally meaningful *as culture*, given the different access by their adherents to education and other taste-shaping resources. This was a democratic position which some aesthetic elites found highly offensive, even barbaric. Gans's book, in fact, was in part motivated by his irritation with some of the "New York intellectuals," who regarded themselves as guardians of elite culture against the onslaughts of mass media. Their earlier distinctions among "brows" had usually been intended to defend the high and derogate the middle and the low—in some cases (Fiedler 1971; Mailer 1957) to derogate the middle even more severely than the low; low culture, at least, had its authenticity to speak in its favor.

Where does that leave us? For one thing, it leaves us with a concept of culture not only differentiated and democratized but relativized as well. What the anthropological tradition of Boas, Benedict, and Margaret Mead did for the relativization of the culture of whole societies, sociology did for the subcultures of groups smaller than a whole society. Where egalitarian individualism could encourage each American to assert (if not to feel) "I'm just as good as you are," the democratized legitimation of subcultures encourages them to assert (if not always to feel) "my (sub)culture is just as good as yours."

5 / CULTURE AND IDEOLOGY

There is a further and perhaps more profound consequence: when ordinary people have learned to speak explicitly of "my" (or "our") culture, it follows that culture has become conscious and, to some extent, therefore, deliberate. That idea, in part, clashes with another persisting theme that conceives of culture as largely implicit, "traditional," deep, and constituted by *presumably* shared and unspoken meanings, a kind of tacit "background knowledge" without which orderly and customary interaction is hardly conceivable (Polanyi 1958; Garfinkel 1967; Goffman 1971; J. Douglas 1967; Mehan 1975; Cicourel 1974). This is the form of culture typically tapped by ethnomethodologists with their superempirical emphasis on "constitutive practices" and their practiced aversion to conventionally reified concepts (see also Bourdieu 1977 on "doxa"). Culture, in this sense, being "organic," intuitive, and hardly conscious, is difficult if not impossible to *argue* about; its very vocabularies, taken for granted, are not readily deployable for intellectual combat. Hence when assumed proprieties are put at risk, argument sometimes turns ugly, emotional, irrational, and doctrinaire. Try asking Jesse Helms *why* he finds photographs of nude children or of homosexuals in flagrante so deeply offensive. Unlike Max Weber, who had a very strong sense of decency but who also understood that his "bourgeois" sense of it was no more valid than anyone else's, the senator might just respond explosively with something like "If you don't already know I can't tell you;" or "If you don't like our way of doing things crawl back under the rock you came from." Any implicit cultural construct can be "deconstructed" if one is motivated to do that. But everyone needs relatively undeconstructed concepts to think with, which is why deconstructing usually has an ideological character.

Take another modest example from common experience: the phrase "peer pressure" is most often invoked in a context of concern over the influence of age-mates on children and youth, perhaps especially with respect to sex and drugs. Usage of the phrase "peer pressure" almost always *assumes* that it is a danger, and the young are typically cautioned to resist it. Resist what exactly? Peer pressure, of course, simply refers to the efforts of one's friends and other contemporaries to exert influence—which is a usually benign and banal aspect of all cultural processes; we try to influence our friends, our friends try to influence us. Why, then, does this routine interactive process take on particularly sinister meaning in the context of secondary schools? Because compulsory mass education has created the conditions in which parents and school authorities must *compete* with students themselves for influence; therefore defining "peer pressure" as sinister is a way of weakening the competition and strengthening an assumption that *only* parents (and other adult authorities) have a *right* to influence children and youth. That is an assumption one may or may not share (Margaret Mead certainly did not share it), but it is difficult even to become conscious of not sharing it until one can break through the linguistic hegemony of "peer pressure."

I think it's worth noting too that "peer pressure" would probably not have attained its negative linguistic power outside a context of compulsory mass education in consolidated urban high schools whose student population is diverse in terms of ethnicity, social class, and culture. Under these conditions the injunction to resist peer pressure can easily be interpreted as a kind of code in which the "good" boys and girls are urged to resist the "bad" (nonwhite, non-middle-class?) kids—which could be a school-bound version of the old practice of blaming "outside agitators" for the troubles in our midst. Deconstructing peer pressure, then, reveals that it is not always less wholesome than parental pressure or the pressure of the school counselor. When it isn't less wholesome it should be easier to recognize that if one is not unconsciously intimidated by the tyranny of language.

A challenge to assumptions is very threatening not only to recurrent ritual practice and customary observance; a critical examination of cultural premises is threatening even to the carefully formulated arguments of professional intellectuals (Kuhn 1962)—and, perhaps, why every professional intellectual bent on theoretical innovation must at some point challenge the assumptions implicit in the "conventional wisdom," conventional because the assumptions (i.e., the tacitly shared and perhaps reified culture) that render it wise have not yet been undermined by the scrutiny of critical reason.

Let us take the argument another step along the way. If cultures are sets of shared meanings associated with customary practices—many of those meanings implicit and dimly, if at all, conscious—then the increasing recognition and legitimation of subcultures gradually reveal our ignorance of groups (and their subcultures) with which we have had no connection or experience. As the ignorance begins to recede (through urbanization and other migration, contact, mass media, education, better communication, and other breachings of social barriers), consciousness of the differences among subcultures is heightened. Liberal pluralists have frequently expressed the hope that such heightened consciousness would increase mutual understanding and tolerance. Earlier in our history, differences among subcultures were far less frequently matters of public knowledge. If they were known, they were muted by physical segregation or other forms of insulation between groups, which ensured only infrequent contact. And when there was contact it was more often than not socially controlled by its hierarchical character, in which subordinate groups either passively accepted (or did not often mount organized protest against) their subordination—although passive resistance and sporadic spontaneous rebellions were not uncommon.

Clearly, however, heightened consciousness of the differences among subcultures can not only enhance mutual understanding and tolerance but may also sharpen the potential or actual conflicts between them. It seems obvious that real differences of culture have been revealed over the last few decades by public policy debates on such issues as school prayer, abortion, affirmative action, quotas, the Equal Rights Amendment, bilingualism, the death penalty, pornography, violence, and other strongly felt "moral" issues. Although some politicians attempt to win support by making such issues salient, most legislators are usually not eager to deal forthrightly with what they call "social" issues. Unlike more narrowly practical "political" and "economic" issues (which involve *divisible* resources like money and other tangible perquisites), "social" issues cannot easily be negotiated in the horse-trading styles with which legislators are experienced and skilled. More than even the debates over popular and elite tastes, these debates over "moral" issues (involving the "deep" values of much larger numbers of people) generate profound "symbolic" meaning and volatile emotionality precisely because they represent claims and counterclaims to the honor and legitimacy of whole ways of life, as well as to who gets how much from the pool of available material resources. Nevertheless, it has become clear that the outcome of such "moral" struggles profoundly affects the status and power of the groups aligned on one or the other side of the issues.

Prohibition was one such issue, cigarette smoking another, abortion a third, homosexuality a fourth. When Prohibition was waxing, someone who, when offered a drink, disdainfully answered "I never touch the stuff," was making a prestige claim that he or she presumed would be honored. A generation later, such a reply to a host's courteous offer would have seemed laughable if not positively ill-mannered. For decades tobacco manufacturers took for granted the effectiveness and success of cigarette advertising campaigns based on the portrayal of smokers as chic, athletic, sophisticated, and attractive. That little chunk of culture is well on its way to oblivion; smoking is already largely a working-class phenomenon. The Marlboro Man-ish trail boss in the film *City Slickers* perhaps drove the last nail into the coffin of that particular image. Kristin Luker has shown how deeply pro-choice and pro-life opinions are embedded in the different ways of life of the women who espouse them, and how much more there is at stake in the abortion controversy than the lives of fetuses. The AIDS plague struck at precisely the historical moment when gay groups had made substantial political gains toward making their way of life culturally tolerable, if not exactly respectable, and there is little doubt that this fact has functioned as a latent subtext in the early foot-dragging on AIDS research funding (Shilts 1987; Gusfield 1962; Luker 1984; Schudson 1984).

In short, one of the consequences of conflict between subcultures is that the assumptions that render routine social practices as "cultural" elements of dignified and meaningful ways of life get revealed. And once revealed, they become *arguable*. When that happens, some of the relationships between conventional culture and the status or power of social groups is also revealed. *It is at this point that culture is transformed into ideology.* The genie is out of the bottle; Pandora's box is open; Humpty Dumpty falls off the wall. Bourdieu's "doxa" is transformed into orthodoxy and heterodoxy. What was but no longer is taken for granted can never again be blithely assumed. Rather, "backlashes" and other efforts to restore the authority of traditional "mainstream" culture or some status quo ante must be argued for. Note the political disaster of the Republican Party's attempt to invoke "traditional family values" (despite the profound changes in the structure and composition of the family over the preceding generation) in the American presidential campaign of 1992. Note also the American military's opposition in 1993 not to gays in military service (that's a fact of life) but to openly and admittedly gay people in the military. The closet discourages argument. Note too the popular furor over "political correctness"—as if the desire to be politically correct were something other than a permanent condition in which all of us are constrained to be mindful of the cultural pieties of the groups with which we are involved.

Under modern political conditions (democratic pluralism), then, ideologies are constant companions to culture. "Ideology" is employed here in its most familiar common usage: ideas that are consciously and deliberately deployed and deployable for "rational" intellectual combat in promoting and defending the legitimacy of group interests and practices (or, at micro-levels of analysis, personal interests and practices). It is worth noting here that I intend this usage as a politically neutral one; ideologies are not *other* people's arguments but all arguments (including the one I am making here), about which there are substantial counterarguments, especially when one of the issues at hand is the legitimacy of the controversy itself.

Nor do I contrast ideology with "truth" or science. Ideology is what replaces taken-for-granted culture when the latter is subjected to critical scrutiny, and hence must be defended with argument. The point is that argument generates counterargument. The reigning philosophy of science seems to me to be a fairly persuasive ideology, although it of course has its critics (see, among many others, Feyerabend 1988; Latour and Woolgar 1979; Latour 1989; Bloor 1991). But this criticism (that science-as-practice is not fully rationalized, and is not independent of social influence) has weakened, if only just a little, the formerly assumed cultural "authority" of science, which must then argue that its distinctive mode of pursuing knowledge can reduce the ignorance that enables opposing arguments to seem plausible to different contituencies. With this formulation, we can expect not "an end to ideology" but a vast increase in it, as former assumptions become more readily and routinely debatable.

The increase in ideology, however, does not necessarily (or even probably) mean a decline in the bulk or amount of shared culture. Unlike oil, culture is a continually renewable resource. The breakup of old chunks of culture may be accompanied by an increase in irritable incivilities and the combat of ideologies, but some ideologies eventually win sufficiently broad support to establish new chunks of culture (see section 6), and habitual new consensuses are generated daily by new situations and circumstances in which interactions gradually become customary: for example, e-mail etiquette. Moreover, some hegemonies always remain unchallenged. Nevertheless, the lines between ideology and culture can be vague and shifting; to the Italian Marxist Antonio Gramsci, the very imputation of culture to a group was an ideological act to the extent that it removed certain "shared" values from the arena of legitimate controversy. This, in a sense, is what Gramsci meant by the "hegemonic" functions of culture; as a Marxist party official, he was interested in reducing the hegemony of bourgeois culture, although he may not have been prepared to understand that any culture requires some hegemony. The transformation or evolution of culture into ideology (i.e., from something commonly taken for granted into something legitimately controversial) weakens such hegemony. It also, of course, risks weakening the thoughtless consensus that makes ordinary civil interaction routine.

This formulation of the relation between "culture" and "ideology" restores some of the dynamic process to the concept of culture that had been calcified by its reified use as a substantive noun (as in "German culture," "American culture," or "Balinese culture"). To the commonplace that culture persistently reproduces itself it adds the banality that culture is always changing; indeed, it must change in some respects in order to reproduce itself in others (Thompson, Ellis, and Wildavsky 1990), and in modern pluralist societies it is deliberately contested. One of the outcomes of the labor-management struggles of the 1930s and 1940s, for example, was management's final recognition of the legitimacy of labor's (including unskilled labor's) right to bargain collectively over wages and working conditions (a cultural change) and labor's acceptance of management's exclusive prerogatives over production policy and the labor process (a cultural continuity). One of the key phases of such continuity and change occurs when, through public policy conflict (in this case the struggle over the Taft-Hartley Act), the interpenetration of taken-for-granted values (cognitive, moral, aesthetic) and the practical political and economic interests of groups is revealed.

6 / CULTURE AND INTERESTS

The revelation of that connection is often regarded as vulgar or coarse (politics in the novel, said Stendhal, is like a pistol shot in the middle of a concert) and is often strongly resisted, especially by those who prefer to think of their "interests" in one realm of discourse and their culture (or values) in quite another. Most people most of the time probably think of their interests as important yet mundane and instrumental matters, perhaps not wholly or candidly mentionable in polite company. "Special interests" is a term with negative connotations despite the fact that every person and group has such interests, which they are expected to pursue. Invoking "special interests" is a sure sign that ideologies are at issue. Is it a contradiction to say that our culture holds special interests in bad repute while, at the same time, recognizing the legitimacy of their pursuit? I think not. What's working here, rather, is the cultural association of the realm of interests with the secular and the worldly—a divisive and conflictful realm about which the culture is properly ambivalent (whereas the realm of values is associated with the sacred, transcendent, and unifying). Note the customary verb usage in these matters: we "seek" values (seeking and seekers have long had good cultural press), but we "pursue" interests, a chase not exactly disapproved of by the culture but not generally ennobled by it either. And we conduct the pursuit through a political process (from family and office politics to national and international politics) against expected opposition and, depending on how vital the interests are conceived to be, using whatever means are possible or necessary, from legitimate ones (sweet talk, persuasion, bargaining, pressure) to quasi-legitimate ones (favors, influence-peddling, arm-twisting, mutual back-scratching) to overtly illegitimate ones (bribery, blackmail, dirty tricks, terrorism, and worse).

In contrast, one tends to thinks of one's culture or "values" as deep, personal, noble, transcendent, even sacred—autonomous properties of one's very being or identity, self-evidently valid to all but fools or knaves, not usually in need of explicit defending against opposition, and negotiable only under the gravest conditions and at the risk of one's sacred honor and even, perhaps, one's sanity. In "idealist" America we say, I'm the sort of person who believes this or that, rather than, I'm the sort of person characterizable as of this time, of that place, commanding these resources and under those constraints. One more of many examples of the conflict between values and interests was sharply revealed in late 1993 when the governing body of a suburban Texas county voted against giving a tax abatement to the Apple Corporation (which planned to build a multimillion dollar facility there) because it morally disapproved of Apple's policy of including gay couples in the benefit package it extended to its employees. In recessionary economic circumstances where investment and job creation were eagerly sought by other Texas jurisdictions, however, the county quickly reversed itself after strong economic and political pressures were brought to bear following the national publicity about its moral disapproval.

That separation of realms of discourse (between persons as creatures of belief and persons as constituted by their place in the social structure) is increasingly blurred and threatened by the revelation of the connections between culture and interests. The threat is there because the persisting referent of culture is to meanings that "we" (all or nearly all of us) symbolically hold in common, whereas the persisting referent of ideology is to meanings, deployed in behalf of "interests," about which "we" disagree. (I intend this "we" to apply to any level of cultural analysis, from families—in which the "we" is inclusive of kin—to the culture of the nation—in which the "we" is inclusive of citizens.) Resistance to the threat is not difficult to understand: the transformation of consensus into sectarianism or dissension can be very troublesome at all levels of social interaction because it erodes the bases for civility and trust and risks anomie. It is nevertheless clear that this is a continuing historical process; the meaning of none of the key terms is fixed over time. Culture breaks up into ideologies (in recent decades, for example, over premarital chastity and the etiquettes of race and gender relations) or almost entirely disappears (the epic as a literary genre, the droit du seigneur, the cadences of Victorian speech); what was once sectarian and ideological (i.e., controversial) wins a widely general cultural consensus (equality of opportunity, marriage for love, expressionist aesthetics, the universal adult franchise); and all such changes occur against opposition rooted in the interests of social groups. What I am suggesting here is that we conceive culture, ideology, and interests as analytic elements of a continuous historical process through which societies, with blood, sweat, and tears, struggle politically toward their conceptions of the true, the beautiful, and the good.

Equality of opportunity, for example, was long opposed by aristocrats and others with the argument that mere competence or technical merit was not a good indicator of "character," the quality most desirable in high positions, and that "breeding" was a far more reliable guarantor of character than talent or merit. Family and clan elders opposed romantic love as grounds for marriage with an argument that marriages arranged by elders in the interests of the political or economic alliance of kin were far more important to family stability and power than (unstable) sexual attraction. The universal adult franchise was opposed by those who argued that property ownership, for example, as an indicator of "responsibility" and a stake in the community, should be a requirement for voting rights. Even the right to some minimum "floor" of welfare payments to those legitimately unable to support themselves now commands a cultural and political near-consensus, whereas not very long ago Social Darwinism, fed by Malthusian ideas about the pointlessness of public support for the poor, was an important, if not dominant, ideology.

Real cultural change is contained in these shifts of public sentiment. But although the arguments in behalf of breeding, arranged marriages, property qualifications for voting, and simply letting the incompetent die and disappear from the gene pool were defeated, public knowledge of just how the defeats occurred is relatively slim. Scholars know something about them, but cultural change, once fully accomplished, makes the once-legitimate but now-defeated ideas seem outlandish, beyond the pale, whereas the success of the ideas that replaced them is seen as the result of their self-evident superiority in moral, cognitive, or aesthetic terms. The bitter conflicts between interest groups over these ideas tend to recede into "history," and we are left with the self-evident and apparently permanent truths of culture.

Nor should we make the mistake of thinking that earlier defeated ideas are "dead." There is no law of progress working here. There is a sense in which ideas seldom metaphorically die. History and circumstance may render them dormant, but if large numbers of people once found them persuasive they conceivably could again if and when history and circumstance can spark them awake. "Ethnic cleansing" in the Balkans reminds us that "ancient blood feuds," far from being a thing of the past, can be made to seem legitimate by political elites using them to stir ethnic hatreds in an effort to consolidate dictatorial power. What would it take to revivify Social Darwinism in public sentiment? When the tax burden on income-earning sectors of the population becomes too great, how many votes could be gathered by a charismatic candidate with arguments that the moral and economic health of the nation would be improved by policies that permitted the unfit, the addicted, the undeserving poor, the habitual criminal, and so on, to be quietly put out of their misery?

There is, I think, a lot of resistance to the effort to connect culture to economy and values to interests, to see their simultaneous relevance to each other rather than to keep them segregated in separate realms of discourse. This resistance obviously stems from that peculiar "idealism" that links one's identity to one's beliefs (and hence protects those beliefs from the morally ambiguous realm of interests) and from that peculiar "individualism" that insists on the self-generation of those beliefs, relieved only by an occasional (and somewhat apologetic) nod to the influence of the family or the church—as in "I was brought up to believe. . ."

But the resistance may also stem from an unthoughtful conception of interests. Albert Hirschman's brilliant little book *The Passions and the Interests* clearly documents changes over time in the meaning of "interests": from a kind of Hobbesian greed, a limitless passion for more, to a kind of *prudent* pursuit, a prudence dictated by the constraints of one's embeddedness in social structure. The uneasy evasion of candor about interests may reflect an ambivalence between both meanings, not unlike the political multivalence of ethnic identity mentioned earlier, and not unlike the similarity of Bourdieu's idea of "systematic misrecognition" (which has a critical/leftish cast) to the conservative idea of "benign ignorance," which is usually offered as an essential component of how traditional social order is maintained and protected against the rational excesses of critical scrutiny.

It may be a mistake to think of interests as permanently given by economic circumstance, as almost redundantly following adjectives like "crass," "vulgar," and "greedy." Mary Douglas and Baron Isherwood in *The World of Goods* and Marshall Sahlins in *Culture and Practical Reason* surely think it a mistake. The assumption that interests are given by economic circumstances (an assumption oddly shared both by hard-headed conservatives and hard Marxists) may indicate the peculiarly modern dominance of economic institutions, and not, as Marxists would have it, a permanent and universal condition of pre-Communist history. According to Sahlins this dominance is, for example, not present in "primitive societies," where interests are given by kinship, which is the dominant institution. For these anthropologists, especially Sahlins, culture is logically prior to economy because culture defines how economic interests are perceived and prioritized. Preferences or tastes, in short, which most economists regard as given, sociologists and anthropologists regard as problematic. Indeed, much of sociology and anthropology is dedicated to the discovery of the *relations* and the direction of causality between cultural preferences or choices and the structurally embedded character of the persons (and groups) who have preferences and make choices.

In *Culture and the Evolutionary Process*, Boyd and Richerson suggest that people need not recognize the objective character of interests in order to pursue them. (Indeed, sometimes not recognizing them enhances the moral "purity" of the pursuit.) Such lack of recognition is often regarded as benign by some traditionalists who see this ignorance as a kind of glue holding society together and protecting it from "pathologies" like anomie and relativism that come from too much conscious rationalism. The opposing view (Sahlins's, for example) about the "subjectivity" of interests has two sources of attractiveness, theoretical and practical. Theoretically, it seems plausible to assert that it takes some cultural judgment to determine and prioritize one's interests. More important, perhaps, the priority of internalized culture to interests functions as a practical guarantee on liberty by making interests a matter of subjective choice rather than the objective "necessity" or probability following from social placement (i.e., the Marxist view—but also the rationalist view). "False consciousness," then, becomes an illegitimate concept. In its place is put the notion that persons are the ultimate judges of their interests, not an objective impersonal theory of social placement or structure.

Neither anthropologists, nor sociologists, nor economists, I fear, have the "last word" in matters like this one. Although Sahlins is persuasive about the role of culture in defining interests, he says little or nothing persuasive (beyond his comments on dominant institutions—which do not cite the original contributions made by Gerth and Mills 1953) about how it is that culture defines interests in the way it does (rather than some other way), for that could well take us back to the causalities pressed *upon* culture by the range of incentives and constraints to which groups are limited by virtue of their locations in economic and social structure. But, Sahlins might retort, "incentives" and "constraints" are not self-evidently "objective," dictated not by a structural position but by a chunk of culture that defines *which* circumstances properly generate incentives and constraints, and which incentives and what constraints are to be understood (and felt) as centrally relevant or "rational," *given* a structural position.

Well, yes, but this is not yet the end of it either. Anthropologists and sociologists want to know, as Sahlins indicates, how culture shapes the very conception of rationality that economists take for granted. If that rationality seems a purely objective matter, it is only the hegemony of the dominant economic institution at work. One theoretical consequence of making preferences problematic is to reveal that hegemony and, by revealing it, to make it arguable, and by making it arguable, perhaps to weaken it. Arguments may be won or lost; the hegemonic is not available to argument.

Moreover, in pluralist societies, where many traditional chunks of culture have broken up into alternative ideologies, legitimations lie about like kindling on the forest floor, gatherable to feed the fires of controversy as *circumstances* mandate. Culture implies/invokes *some* legitimation, but in pluralist societies, *which* legitimations are found or invoked depends upon the circumstances and the interests of those requiring them. The idea (indeed the cliché) of "quality time" as a legitimating feature of child rearing, for example, was not found (or required) until mothers began to be present in large numbers in the paid labor force, and needed an argument warranting their status as "good mothers," despite the reduced amount of time they could spend with their children. Note, however, that the desideratum of "good mother" remained culturally intact in spite of the fact that we reliably know rather little about the relation between specific child-rearing practices and their developmental consequences for children. Or, to use another example, when members of Congress grant favors to influential campaign contributors are they "selling out" the American people or "serving their constituents"? The legitimating and the delegitimating arguments are equally available, and the groups likely to select one or the other may be "sincere" in their beliefs yet fairly predictable at the same time. Interests and legitimating arguments are seldom strangers to each other.

7 / MATERIAL AND IDEAL INTERESTS

Let's go back now to Weber's reference to material and ideal interests, a distinction clearly parallel to his more famous distinction between "class" (life chances in economic markets) and "status" (quantum of honor embedded in and imputed to a style of life). The latter distinction was no doubt in part intended as an effort to save some autonomy for the realm of status (i.e., culture—although Weber did not consistently use that term in this context) against predominantly Marxist efforts to "reduce" matters of prestige or honor to matters of class and material interests.

In this formulation, then, "ideal interests" are those largely symbolic goods that certify the honor of a style of life or course of action to which a person's identity or self-esteem is committed by virtue of his or her participation in or identification with groups bearing that style of life. "Material interests," on the other hand, refer largely to those goods that maintain or enhance one's life chances in the market. But remember Sahlins's (and Mary Douglas's) point: what enhances or sustains one's life chances in the market are culturally defined. And remember Bourdieu, much of whose work is dedicated to the analysis of *relations* between class and status, hence to connections between styles of life and life chances in the market, thus to the linkages between ideal and material interests. Bourdieu's most important contribution here is the idea of cultural capital. Whatever its ambiguities (its relation to social or aesthetic or educational capital—he uses all these terms), the idea of capital (resources deployable in markets for one's own gain) can usefully be extended from economic to cultural resources (titles, credentials, style, social skills). Cultural capital, like economic capital, is (1) deployable in status markets to maintain or enhance the honor of one's position in it, and (2) constitutes a *currency*, again like economic capital, transformable or exchangeable into other forms of advantage (or disadvantage). Penniless European aristocrats marrying the daughters of American plutocrats combines honor and money. "Reputation," for example, may also function in this way, as a tradable or negotiable commodity.

How are ideal interests related to material interests? In ways that range from the obvious to the subtle to the elusive. It is obvious, for example, that whereas everyone may be said to have ideal interests in "free speech" (the legitimacy of First Amendment rights), professional intellectuals (journalists, professors, the clergy, politicians, etc.) have a far more *vital* ideal interest than the kinds of ordinary citizens who may seldom have occasion to use that freedom in public forums—and who have been shown by opinion polls to be ready to deny First Amendment rights to certain despised minorities (Stouffer 1955). Somewhat more subtle is the ideal interest that ethnic and other minority groups have in legitimating cultural pluralism or multiculturalism, which not only enhances the honor of their subcultures and (presumably) their self-esteem, but also enhances their chances to pursue material interests in economic markets by reducing prejudice and discrimination against them. More elusive are the circumstances described by Chandra Mukerji (1989) in which senior scientists, federally funded, have material interests in maintaining their labs and those employed in them but also have ideal interests in advancing their science and the particular lines of research they are conducting, irrespective of the government's interest in the bearing of the research on the *applied* problems for which the research was funded. Are the material interests of scientists connected to their ideal interests? In some ways certainly: the government's funding of practical research enables the scientists to pursue "pure" science and to hone their research skills (the government wants such skills in reserve, ready to be invoked in case of national emergency), and their achievements in basic science enhance both their prestige within the subculture of scientists *and* their life chances in the particular section of the labor market in which they work. There are trade-offs there, of course, and the details of the accounting may not be entirely clear. What is clear, however, is that the effort to find connections between ideal and material interests weakens the grounds for conceiving ideal and material interests (like culture and economy more generally) as belonging to separate and autonomous realms of discourse.

That effort is often conducted against vigorous opposition. Even to speak of material interests in a discussion of culture evokes "materialism," which, in turn, evokes Marxism for many, and there has been a tendency over the past decade or so simply to dismiss analytic concepts that have been associated with Marxist habits of thought. "Reductionism," for example (as I said earlier and of which I will say more below), is now frequently used as little more than a pejorative. Similarly, to use the concept of "false consciousness" is now frequently dismissed as having no analytic merit—despite more than adequate evidence that we human beings are frequently expert at self-delusion (Barnes 1994). "Conspiracy theory" is currently in sufficiently bad cultural repute that one feels constrained to distance oneself from anything that sounds remotely like it—although that powerful persons meet privately to plan policies and actions affecting us all is something, I take it, that no one will bother to deny. Finally, "interest theory" applied to culture is often dismissed as overly simple (Schudson 1989) or, worse, reductionist—especially when ideals, values, or other symbolic commitments are seen as being "reduced" to interests.

In one sense these dismissive tendencies are not difficult to understand: the individualist idealism of Americans is offended by any effort that seeks to understand it by connecting it to external matters. On the other hand, questions about the *relation* of ideals to material circumstances seem to invite themselves in a pluralist world in which multiple ideals are made available and accessible: how is it that one believes A rather than B when both seem plausible, available, and are supported by substantial constituencies of believers?

"Interest theory" is simple only when vulgarized for transparent polemical purpose. It's not so simple when, in addition to gross class interests, one includes equally material interests rooted in ethnicity, gender, or family (which may diverge from class interests), or the interests generated by placement in what Bourdieu calls "fields" (institutional/occupational milieux), each of which can then be conceived as relatively autonomous variables interacting in distinctly unsimple-to-discover patterns. Nor are even blatant economic interests exactly irrelevant; rather, it's easy for intellectuals to get, well, bored with class analysis and "interests." Like Freudian psychoanalysis, Marxist habits of analysis have trickled down sufficiently into the popular culture that any reading of the original texts is no longer required in order to see unconscious motives and class interests lurking in ordinary behavior. The disdain for such analytic practice, then, is perhaps less a matter of its "simplicity" than a case of familiarity breeding contempt. Among intellectuals, after all, to say that something is more complicated than it appears is a truism to which all assent. Complexity makes work for intellectuals, and that life is almost always more complex than our analytic categories permit us to comprehend is no doubt true, but not in itself a devastating critique of those categories.

Finally, to see symbolic commitments as "ideal interests" is to suggest that an entire mode of life is associated with their maintenance; it also provides one with a set of analytic tools for reducing the mystery of why this rather than that chunk of culture is salient and for solving the riddle of who believes what for which reasons. Symbolic commitments, of course, usually vary in patterned ways, depending on social placement, and it should be no surprise that ideal and material interests typically reinforce each other. The surprise—even chagrin—is when they don't. It should be no shock that religious officials, for example, are likely to have strong commitments to the inviolability of the realm of the sacred; nor that journalists claim the right to protect the anonymity of their sources; nor that professors invoke academic freedom; nor that adolescents and post-adolescents, reared for the most part in the "ideal culture" of their society and as yet relatively unbound by practical ties to careers, household, or community, have a tendency to be morally preachy and to be shocked—shocked!—by the hypocrisies of their elders.

The empirical interpenetration, then, of ideal and material interests should be less an offense to individualist idealism than a reassurance that one's connection to the culture is working "normally." It is only when the self-serving pursuit of material interests is bereft of and unlegitimated by any symbolic commitments that we are likely to speak pejoratively of arrogance, acquisitiveness, brutality, or greed. And it is only when an unbending devotion to a moral ideal is not grounded in (and restrained by) practical ties to the materiality of an everyday life that we are likely to see that devotion as fanaticism or zealotry. Max Weber knew a lot about the latter, enough to be more than skeptical about what he called an "ethic of ultimate ends." But if complexity is an intellectual virtue, it's worth pointing out that Weber's preference for an "ethic of responsibility" was itself a preference held with sufficient passion to approach becoming an "ultimate end" of its own.

8 / CULTURE, INTERESTS, POLITICS

Interests, then, are not quite the same as primitive wants or desires or even "necessity." A capitalist's "greed for" profit is not the same as his or her "interests in" profit. The latter requires an argument, a set of ideas that *justifies* profit (here, Sahlins would see culture defining interests), by its asserted relation to investment and employment, for example, and hence to the general welfare or "the public interest." The term "public interest" suggests that interests are not necessarily "special"—or not exclusively special. At any given moment most of the public interest (beyond that which is culturally taken for granted) is up for ideological grabs. An essential feature of ideologies as political weapons is that the private or special interests generating them make claims that they serve the public interest as well.

These claims may be made more or less persuasively, and be backed by greater or lesser power. Some ideological work (Berger 1981) draws more effectively than other such work from the common stock of extant culture, but it's a tricky operation in part because at any given moment it may not be clear how widely shared a chunk of culture actually is. Some thirty-five years ago, when Charles Wilson of General Motors, articulating what he apparently took to be the culture of capitalism, allegedly made his famous remark that "what's good for General Motors is good for the United States," many, perhaps most, Americans did not find it persuasive, but offensive, even arrogant. What he thought was the culture of capitalism turned out to be an ideology, not as widely shared as he thought. The word "capitalism" was not in the best of repute, and the Advertising Council sponsored a national contest at that time to find a more benign (commercial?) name for "the American economic system." Even today, in a far more conservative period, the phrase "market economy" is generally preferred to "capitalism" as a less controversial category of thought.

On the other hand, the claim of physicians, lawyers, scientists, and university professors for exclusive autonomy to define the standards of professional competence, although surely serving their "special interests" (material and ideal), has also won a much broader consensus that it serves the general interest as well—although, particularly in recent years, the inherent biases of "objective" criteria of competence have been challenged by minorities.

Both culture and ideology, then, invoke values; indeed, "ideological" values are sometimes felt more intensely, precisely because, more directly tied to material interests than "cultural" values, they tend to inspire opposition. This disparity is especially evident when "cultural" values, as ideal interests, are made to seem ethereal, autonomous, even transcendent, that is, unconnected to real interests—sometimes, indeed, banal, as in the idealizations of home, mother, and apple pie. The difference, as I have been trying to make clear, is in how widely, and among whom specifically, values are shared (and their consequent implications for civil peace or conflict).

The problems that persons have with the relations between their ideology and their culture usually involve integration or consistency, or "fit." Such problems are not limited to minorities or other groups whose marginal social status creates problems of access to the dominant culture—for example, the teenage heavy metal "burnouts" in Donna Gaines's *Teenage Wasteland*, who are habitually truant from high school, into illegal drugs and alcohol, and yet adore Ronald Reagan. In *Habits of the Heart*, the authors describe a small-town Chrysler dealer, a local notable and normally a free-market Republican, who makes a passionate speech to a service club in 1982 defending the federal government's bailout of the then-troubled Chrysler Corporation, and denouncing as nearly treasonous the purchase of foreign cars by Americans in a disastrously depressed American car market. Although it would be easy enough to see it as cynically self-serving (see Bailey 1983), the speech, apparently oblivious to the contradiction between free-market ideology and the "buy American" interests at hand, was deeply and sincerely felt. Obviously a great deal is "working" here: not only a complex mix of culture, ideology, and interests, but also the car dealer's institutionally embedded status as a prestigious town father, a Prominent Citizen threatened with disaster by economic developments utterly beyond his control. Under such conditions, almost anyone would reach out desperately, even anarchically, for whatever resources of righteousness might be found, and damn the consistency.

Liberals and relativists tend to see a minimum quantum of shared culture, a sort of "rules of the game," within which they can preach their ideological diversities and practice their different strategies ("life styles") for playing the game. There are of course limits here, although they are elastic. Consistently predictable "losers" in the game played according to extant rules may sometimes blame themselves but may also be said to have "interests in" changing or junking the rules by which they become consistent and predictable losers (hence, for example, civil disobedience, guerilla tactics, ghetto gangs, terrorism, etc.). Liberals tend to be relatively weak in situations of moral confrontation because their "cultural" values, being primarily procedural and secular, inhibit them from proclaiming any absolute knowledge of right and wrong. And if Richard Rorty is correct that, for a liberal, being cruel is the worst thing one can do, there's another reason for avoiding confrontation. Confrontation often induces, even requires, cruelty to one's antagonists.

Fundamentalists tend to see culture more strongly—although they don't usually call it culture. Derived mostly from sacred books, their value-claims are authoritative, universal, and orthodox, and their almost exclusively *moral* discourse is apparently disembodied of "interests" except those so presumably taken for granted that they hardly seem like interests: for example, the sanctity of the "traditional" family or the holiness of the Founders. Knowing the difference between right and wrong, their metier is moral confrontation. Ideologies are not seen as justifications of permissible diversities, more or less reasonable from the points of view of those who assert them, but as the voice of the Devil, of decadence, of sin, ruinous to the moral fibre of the nation or community, and not to be tolerated. Marxists often partake of both views. Out of power, they tend to see mostly interest-tied ideology (the ruling ideas of an age are the ideas of the ruling class); in power, they tend to limit or suppress ideological diversity—though sometimes not much more than in the U.S., where legitimate political positions cover a rather narrow ideological range. An innocent American visitor to France, for example, may be surprised to see both Communist and near-fascist spokespersons as regular panel members on TV talk shows discussing the political issues of the day.

As more and more self-evident culture is transformed into contentious ideologies by a challenge to its assumptions, by deconstructions of its implicit categories, or by revelations of the connections between ideal and material interests, politics gets more rancorous. The Left (representing claims for new legitimacies and entitlements by increasingly aggressive and formerly subordinate groups) and the Right (representing the claims of groups formerly confident of the unchallenged hegemony or centrality of their culture—but now increasingly besieged) are having at each other in political struggles—over public policy issues to be sure, but with not-so-hidden agendas that implicate whole ways of life. The culture wars are now an apparently permanent part of the social process, and ideological work has become a major occupation.

When, therefore, we Americans ask ourselves what holds us together as one nation, one people, an answer that invokes "traditional" culture or once-hegemonic symbols (Uncle Sam, the Stars and Stripes, the Alamo, the Liberty Bell, Washington, Jefferson, Lincoln, the fruited plain, the twilight's last gleaming) must seem to some increasingly attenuated: thin, abstract, decontextualized, "ideological." If, as Jesse Unruh reportedly said, "money is the mother's milk of politics," then ideology is its Banana Rice Cereal, but culture is its meat and potatoes. We need all three to nourish the body politic, but we need them in different recipes at different times. Where the Founding Fathers could confidently proclaim for posterity that they held certain truths to be self-evident ("self-evident truths," as distinguished from "scientific truths," is, of course, another way of referring to culture), we scholars are now more likely to be impressed by the hard bargaining that went into revealing those self-evident truths than by the confident eloquence of the consensus with which they were finally asserted in the Declaration of Independence, one of our most sacred documents. What holds us together, then, may in retrospect be a common culture, but if so, it is a common culture forged in a here and now by the bargains we have struck, the compromises we have achieved, and, where these have failed, by the demonstrations we have mounted, the social movements we have spawned, the wars we have fought, the victories we have won, the defeats we have suffered, and even, perhaps, the corruptions we are left with.

9 / PLURALISM AND CONSENSUS

Nothing I have said so far should be taken to mean that the culture we may be presumed to share is limited to subgroups bound by ethnicities, churches, occupations, classes, families, leisure interests, or some combination of these and yet other partial solidarities. Nor, despite the apparent attenuation of some traditional hegemonic symbols, do I intend to convey that our sense of a national culture is weak. To the contrary, I presume that most of us from time to time sense a national consensus that links our obvious diversities. Tourists sometimes sense it when they meet compatriots in foreign lands. Major political parties try to tap elements of a national consensus in election years, and wars often produce an orgy of consensus-building rhetoric—usually at the most primitive or elemental levels—to induce or enhance "morale" in a national emergency, and to dampen or intimidate dissent by invoking the life-and-death priorities of our troops at the front.

It is ironic that opinion polling, which tries to get at such elements of a national consensus, often reveals only how volatile, fluctuating, and ad hoc opinion is. If there were any lasting or consistent relation between a general cultural consensus and its application to specific issues, weekly opinion polls would hardly be necessary, nor their results so variable, given slight changes in the wording of questions or "spin" comment on developing events by the media and other interested parties. Still, if those consensual elements are there, it seems important that they be discovered, or re-discovered, so that the self-evident truths we in fact still share (or which have newly—and perhaps silently—emerged along the way) may be stated or newly restated in heart-thumping ways that need not embarrass even the least sentimental among us.

They may not be easy to find. If efforts to invoke a consensus are often primitive or manipulative, it is also true that there has been a mean-spirited dimension to our pluralism that has been evident in our politics since the end of World War II—an image in which the body politic appears as an inert carcass that "we" (all of us "special interests") pecked away at, intent on getting ours; and as if the alternative image of republican virtue, the general interest, the common good were so much pap, an empty and withered breast dragged out and offered up to hungry innocents at rallies, photo-ops, inaugural addresses, nominating conventions, and other such ceremonial occasions.

For the purposes of understanding culture (and at the risk of asserting the innocuous) such images are better investigated than doctrinally proclaimed. If the body politic is simply prey (with respect to which the fundamental rule is: get as much as you can however you can), it seems important that this be discovered and widely diffused—if only to help increase the equality of predator-opportunity; equality of opportunity, after all, does seem to be a widely shared element of culture in the U.S. Predatory opportunity is also widely misunderstood. It is likely that the poor ("welfare cheaters," for example) defraud taxpayers far less than their more affluent and sophisticated fellow citizens do (for example, the still unindicted beneficiaries of the S & L scandal), if only because the affluent have far greater structured opportunity to do so. They often do not even have to defraud us since they may legally reach into our collective pockets. Third-class mailing privileges, one of scores of examples, constitute a substantial subsidy for advertisers (have you noticed the bulk of your junk mail in recent years?), which ordinary letter writers pay for with increased rates for first-class mail. On the other hand, if there is a common good out there, it surely needs finding, and, found, needs reaffirming by those who wish to continue to speak as if we shared a common culture.

To say even this, however, can be misleading. Although I have no doubt that there are elements of culture very widely shared by almost all Americans, they are not simply *there*, waiting to be discovered. They are being made and remade every day as the waxing and waning of contentiousness weakens or sustains consensus. And when we try to find out how we construct and reconstruct the symbolic, what we are likely to discover are more or less inconsistent and even contradictory (but patterned) efforts to use *accessible traditions* of legitimation (i.e., culture) in combination with the au courant ideologies at hand to confer some dignity and coherence on the problem-solving courses of action set for us by the ad hoc circumstances we are more or less stuck in.

I think that this is as true for the president of the United States as it is for you and me. The variety of reasons President Bush offered in the autumn of 1990 for his massive deployment of troops in the Persian Gulf (aggression, oil, jobs, nuclear threat, Saddam Hussein as madman or Hitler, etc.) may be regarded as serial efforts to tap a consensus he hoped (but could not be sure) would be there—backed by whatever current ideologies he could reach for, in order to deal with circumstances he was stuck in, and which grew out of the absence of a coherent foreign policy for the Middle East. Not that the Iraqi invasion of Kuwait would not have happened had we a "coherent foreign policy," but its probability would have been reduced, and our own response-options would have been a bit broader than sanctions or all-out war.

Such circumstances not only structure the range of possible solutions we can opt for, but also (given limited resources) indicate in principle the probable choices among the options left before us. It is worth noting that the relatively high level of abstraction in this formulation is intended to be inclusive of "we" as individuals conducting interpersonal relations and "we" as official role-players acting for collectivities and oriented to publics, markets, or constituencies. This formulation, then, should be applicable to a wide range of research problems in the sociology of culture.

10 / CULTURE AND EXPERIENCE

In *The Last Intellectuals*, Russell Jacoby's main thesis is that the generation of intellectuals now in their late sixties or older are the "last" intellectuals in perhaps two senses: that of an older or previous generation beyond its prime, and that of the *final* group who can properly be called "intellectuals" in the sense that came down from that word's first French usage in the Dreyfus affair. Jacoby means men and women of letters and politics, usually (though not always) of the liberal Left, who lived and wrote largely independent of permanent salaried connections with big institutions (novelists, poets, essayists, editors of small papers or magazines, free-lance journalists, private scholars, etc.) and who communicated, usually drawing on *their own experience* but often using other sources as well, in a language accessible to large audiences.

Beginning in the mid-to-late 1950s, goes Jacoby's argument, the bulk of the "next" generation who might have become intellectuals (in the sense that Edmund Wilson, Lewis Mumford, I. F. Stone, Mary McCarthy, Susan Sontag, or Dwight MacDonald were intellectuals) instead became academics who, trained in scholarly disciplines, lost or never had the ability to speak in a common language, and who therefore lost their contact with and influence on large publics. Substituted were small audiences of colleagues for whom they wrote in specialized languages, published in academic "journals" (the distinction with magazines is important to academics; one's writings get "refereed" in academic journals rather than paid for), and understood only or primarily by those trained in the specialized languages. Universities reward academics for "technical" achievements and are skeptical of the common language as an imprecise and possibly vulgar attempt at popularization. Hence the system in which professors of humanities, arts, and social sciences are involved abets and encourages the disappearance of intellectuals (and their replacement by "experts").

Nathan Glazer, one of the prominent "last intellectuals" (although he, like some other intellectuals, came indirectly and relatively late to academic life, and has pursued a university career for many years now) says in a recent autobiographical essay (1990) that almost all his writings come out of his own experience. He was a city boy and he wrote about cities and urbanism. He was an ethnic Jew and he wrote about ethnicity.

He was a socialist-Zionist in his youth and wrote about left-wing politics. In his book Jacoby does *not* talk about the apparent decline in the *relevance* of personal experience to one's capacity to say anything interesting or important about the general issues of culture or society, issues that personal experience used to, or was thought to, illuminate. Writing or speaking in a personal voice, citing the evidence of one's own (presumably common) experience is today regarded by most of the academic successors to the last intellectuals as a weak, even trivial, form of argument, and the so-called evidence is demeaned as "anecdotal," that is, not evidence at all. The net result, except for artists, perhaps, is to render experience a sort of illegitimate intellectual resource, and therefore to engender distrust of one's own experience as something from which analytic inferences of general cultural import can properly be made. A gap is thus created between culture-as-experience, between meanings absorbed from living, and the prospect of legitimately using that experience to sustain, enliven, and illumine the cultural dialogue.

That artists are largely exempt from this proscription on the relevance of personal experience may help explain the increasing emphasis on the "art" in ethnography and cultural criticism. In a recent interview, the *New Yorker's* retired movie critic Pauline Kael comments disdainfully on the "saphead objectivity" of the efforts by her editors and outraged readers to induce her to modify her experiential approach to film criticism and her slangy personal style (involving the use of "you" and "we" to suggest that her response to a film was—or should be—the common one). For Kael, film touches too many deep, even unconscious, psychic dimensions to be adequately understood "objectively." In her current work, called *Resident Alien* (forthcoming), the sociologist and art historian Janet Wolff includes far more than film in her efforts to use personal experience to illumine the meanings of rock music, opera, dance, and the metaphors of travel.

I don't wish to be nostalgic about this. Replacing experience as a basis for thinking are consciously constructed conceptual or statistical categories designed in the first place as a means of comprehending the variability and complexity of events and experiences, and as a corrective or control on the inherent biases of any personal angle of vision. This essay is, in part, an example of that transformation, although I have not, as should be clear, entirely given up on the relevance of personal experience. There is, to be sure, a viable logic to this putative transformation of cognitive modes in which the insights gleaned from personal experience become, at best, perhaps a source of hypothesis but clearly not of "knowing." Still, any sociologist of culture "knows" that transformations of cognitive modes do not generally occur through the ethereal power of logics themselves. Logics, like any other successful chunks of culture, have material and social correlates that function as sources of their power or persuasiveness. In this case the sources are not unrelated to the ones cited by Jacoby in his analysis of the last intellectuals. The very size of collectivities, the scope and magnitude of corporate and other institutional enterprises (and their markets) dwarf the relevance of personal experience to the analysis of anything that goes on inside or outside of them. When Kael says that friendship is unlikely between two people who disagree too often about films, I think she is right— although fighting a rear-guard action. With very large enterprises too much is at stake, constituencies are too varied, interests too delicately balanced to valorize or privilege analysis of them based on personal experience rather than on "systematically" gathered evidence by duly certified experts credentialed to gather it. Hence, the "last" intellectual mode is increasingly marginalized or made eccentric. The "last intellectuals," with their literary sensibilities and their left-leaning politics, seemed to many increasingly anachronistic and irrelevant in an imperial nation like the U.S.

This is not to say that "public" intellectuals, in Jacoby's sense, have disappeared; far from it. It is only to say that they are much more heterogeneous and dispersed (not just from New York) and, with some important exceptions, not primarily literary or left-leaning any longer. I'm thinking of "Beltway" intellectuals and columnists, McNeil-Lehrer pundits, experts, spokespersons, and the "northeast corridor" commuters between Boston, New York, and Washington, who change with each federal administration. As a major capitalist world power, the U.S. could hardly tolerate for very long a situation in which its major intellectuals continued to be literary socialists who wrote from their own experience. Today's intellectuals usually have strong mass media connections (Koppel, Will, Buckley), national syndication, think-tank affiliations, strong academic credentials in area or regional studies and polling analysis, and, conservative or not, usually remain well within the currently dominant (and relatively narrow) political consensus.

The *particularity* of experience in a highly differentiated society of subcultures, and the fragile uncertainty of the claims it might make to represent the *common* experience of large numbers of others differently placed, extends all the way from the realm of politics to the popular culture in general and to stand-up comedy in particular. The apparent decline in the relevance of primary experience to a common culture is evident in the styles of American comedians, the best of whom are described as "brilliant" probably more often than professional intellectuals are, and among whom something revealing is happening.

There are increasingly two kinds of stand-up comedians: what can be called the mass-culture comedians (Bob Hope, Johnny Carson, Jay Leno, Joan Rivers) and the subculture comedians (Richard Pryor, Lily Tomlin, George Carlin—at least at earlier stages of their careers). The mass-culture comedians use mass media as a source of comedic material. Aiming at the mass audience, they assume that the only experience the mass audience has in common (hence from which meaningfully comic material can be drawn) is mass-mediated experience (current news headlines, blockbuster movies, hit TV series, national advertising, etc.). When a Jay Leno joke falls flat in his opening five-minute monologue it is usually because he has miscalculated the audience's familiarity with the current news reference he has invoked; people are reading newspapers less. Aiming at smaller audiences, the subculture comedians still rely more on what they take to be the direct life-experience of the audience (which the comedian assumes he or she shares) rather than the secondary or vicarious experience of media. David Letterman is interesting in part because, although he uses media as material, his snide and sarcastic style is "hip," not wholesome and likeable in the image that Jay Leno cultivates, and he assumes a certain level of sophistication or cynicism in his audience if they are to "get" his style. The "late-night" (i.e., early morning) audience apparently got it. But in pitting Letterman against Leno at an earlier time, CBS is betting millions of dollars that hip cynicism is no longer a piece of age-graded marginal subculture for night owls but something the post-local-news mass audience is ready for. If they are not, expect David Letterman to get more wholesome.

The two categories of mass-culture and subculture comedians, then, are not neat, and it is possible to move between them—more than possible since most comedians, as employed professionals, want larger audiences and the greater opportunity that implies for more work at higher pay. But the move carries with it risk and the prospect of changed material; the blunt language and the preoccupations with sex and drugs characteristic, for example, in showrooms and comedy clubs would not pass the TV network censors. George Carlin, a subculture comedian originally, lost some of his old public and changed his material as he got more popular. Others, like Eddie Murphy and Robin Williams, become so successful that their careers get split between movie stardom for the mass audience and live concert performances (rare now) for their original (smaller, hipper) audiences. Still others, like Jonathan Winters, Pryor, and the late John Belushi, run into serious psychological (let alone legal) difficulties as the tensions mount between their subcultural orientations and their increasing mass success. Bill Cosby, of course, is a category with a single occupant. Originally a subculture comedian relying for comic material on the direct experience of his audience, his comedy was so wry, rueful, accepting, and unthreatening that his Apollonian image could smoothly encompass the mass audience where it now resides as almost a paradigm of gentle wisdom, humor, generosity, and tolerance (rather like a contemporary Will Rogers). It need hardly be added that one of the major points of transition between comedy based on the direct common experience of comedian and audience and comedy based on mass media images is the growing reliance on stereotyped or reified experience.

Let me emphasize, again, that in making these "critical" remarks about American comedy, I intend something more than a cultural interpretation of what is happening in it, which readers will find more—or less—persuasive than other interpretations. I intend also to suggest that the major cultural challenge for mass media as publicly responsible institutions is continually to search for newly emerging chunks of shared culture that, although perhaps originating in the experience of small or marginal groups, have gradually become meaningful, moving, or amusing to audiences large enough to interest national advertisers on TV or other investors in mass-marketed culture.

One of the important features of recent culture, represented in "thirtysomething," for example, is how lasting friendships, formed perhaps in school or college, may replace kinship ties with an older generation (significantly weak in "thirtysomething"; almost nonexistent in "Northern Exposure") as a source of primary solidarity. Blood may no longer be thicker than water when the blood thins and the waters are increasingly muddied. On the other hand, the brilliance of "All in the Family" lay in its ability to locate *within* the family many of the volatile controversies dividing the larger society at the time (race, gender, drugs, hippies, the Vietnam War) and to accommodate them through the family in ways that enabled its audiences to sympathize with any of the major characters with whom they were predisposed to identify, while recognizing the controversies as *within* the range of permitted disagreement, containable in the family.

Not all mass-marketed culture, of course, succeeds in making new kinds of solidarity broadly visible (and affirming it) or in legitimating conflict by creating sympathies for all parties to it. Such aims are not often attempted, and when attempted, are not always successful, either aesthetically or commercially. More typical is reliance on well-established formula and conventional stereotypes of ordinary domesticities, or the melodrama of vicariously (beyond the direct experience of most of the audience) exciting milieux (cops, lawyers, doctors) where life-and-death matters are portrayed as routine, although in fact they are not. Richard Hoggart's comment of thirty-five years ago (vis-à-vis his London working-class childhood) still seems apt: that much mass-produced culture is offensive less because it falsifies experience than because it makes the authentic experience of its audiences seem remote and unreal, merely private, even secret, publicly unrepresentable, and hence such experience is largely missing from the historical record.

11 / SOCIOLOGY AND CULTUROLOGY

In the view being emphasized here, a sociology of culture is based on a single fundamental premise: that the meanings contained in and conveyed by distinctive cultural forms are reproduced, survive, persist with only minor modifications or undergo basic changes, *only* through the action of groups (or "networks") of persons who "carry" (or fail to carry) culture from one generation to the next. When eight and nine year olds in a school "Spring Sing" perform a medley of "Get Happy" and "Great Day" complete with showbiz gestures, I find myself moved to involuntary tears—not by the skill of the performance but by the miracle of cultural transmission occurring right in front of me. My daughter is surprised—and pleased—that I know those songs.

A sociology of culture, then, must of course identify the ideas and meanings the forms of whose persistence and change it seeks to understand; but it must also identify the persons and groups, situated in time and place, whose changing constraints and incentives do or do not adequately provide opportunities and motivation to carry those meanings successfully through time—perhaps, even probably, against the motivated opposition of others, differently situated.

To think of persons as "carriers" of culture immediately suggests an analogy to contagious disease, carried in the blood and on the breath, in the minds and on the backs of living sufferers staggering through time. As I have been attempting to frame it here, an empirical sociology of culture is the ethnographic and/or historical study of the ways in which identifiable groups of people, historically situated in conditions they did not entirely choose (hence to some extent stuck with those conditions), produce, reproduce, and alter symbolic meanings through participation in recurrent ritual practice, through stratified institutional forms, and through the clash of subcultures in which what is ultimately at stake is the very character of what the dominant culture "is."

By defining a sociology of culture in this manner I intend to distinguish it from other kinds of cultural studies (I sometimes call them culturologies) that typically devote a great deal of attention to interpreting meanings from symbolic patterns but little or no attention to the contingencies of social structure and their effects on cultural forms and on the actual distribution of symbolic culture in sentient human groups. Instead, culturology spends its analytic efforts reading meaning into cultural forms, with (Freud, Lévi-Strauss, Greimas) or without (much of literary criticism and "cultural studies") an explicit interpretive apparatus. Many have, for example, interpreted the meanings of the "western" film in American culture by focusing on its icons, its myths, its symbolisms, its archetypes, without ever attending to the fact that the mythic "cowboy" is a "farm worker" to the Bureau of Labor Statistics or that a Hollywood film is an industrial product, shaped as much by the constraints of commerce and by the social structure of the industry as by the cultural conventions of the genre or the artistic intentions of the director (Wright 1975).

The difference is clearly connectable to the distinction between *Geisteswissenschaften* and *Naturswissenschaften*. The primarily interpretive work is "humanistic" in character; when asked how they know what they claim to know, interpretive analysts are likely to invoke a "coherence" theory of truth: they take bits and pieces of the cultural "evidence" and infer or construct from them meaningful wholes that are more or less coherent and intellectually and/or aesthetically "compelling"—in quotes only because it is seldom entirely clear exactly what compels assent. The confirmation of one's own unexpressed intuitions? Insight? Freshness? "The shock of recognition"? Lucid arrangement of evidence? Style? All of the above, perhaps. When encountering undeniable brilliance in cultural criticism or interpretive culturology we don't often repress our gratitude by sourly asking what makes it "compelling." Like Garcia Marquez's thing-not-yet-named, we can only helplessly point— and perhaps say yes, do it like that if you're going to do it at all. But not everyone does it like that—which is probably why less-than-compelling interpretation generates endless discussion.

It's worth pointing out here that "rhetoric" used to refer to the arts of persuasion, although today, in a science-dominated cognitive environment, "rhetoric" almost always has an implicit "mere" in front of it, suggesting that any mode of persuasion that goes beyond logic and evidence (which, rigorously speaking, are elements of rhetoric, i.e., persuasion) is empty or illegitimate; hence "mere rhetoric" (style, sentiment, emotional force) means, in the epistemology of science, mostly smoke and mirrors; aesthetic seduction or moral passion substituting for logic and evidence as a way of making what you want to say believable to others: audiences shouting "I care!" to Tinkerbell when, at her faintest, she needs it the most.

That's not easy to achieve. Artists struggle for it, and politicians are usually quite bad at it, immersed as they almost always are in the language of mendacity and opportunism. Lyndon Johnson and George Bush were never *less* "compelling," never more false than when their eyes would go all soft and caring in their efforts to reach out to the common folk on television. Ronald Reagan was better at aesthetic seduction, but then he was indeed an artist of sorts, at least a professional actor for much of his life, skilled at face-work and at the reading of scripts written by others. And, as Truman Capote liked to say of actors in general, Reagan was very likely simpleminded enough (unlike Johnson or Bush) to believe many of the scripts that were written for him.

Richard Nixon was another case entirely. When, at one point in his presidency, he nominated to the Supreme Court a man who was widely considered to be a legal mediocrity, one of Nixon's supporters defended the nomination not by exaggerating the credentials of the nominee but by arguing that most Americans are mediocre (the law of the normal curve?) and that they deserved a representative on the high court. Now there was an argument, a genuinely arresting piece of ideological work! Arresting because its implicit populism was unusual for the Nixon administration (and its supporters), which was generally more comfortable with experts and other elites accomplished in using the language of logic and evidence. And arresting because the argument seemed at the time so *outrageous* that there was not much reasoned argument against it—although the nomination was eventually not confirmed by the Senate.

Sociologists of culture who conceive their work as part of a scientific (rather than humanistic) tradition, are less likely to focus on interpretive work than on the ways in which the patterns and contingencies of social placement either "stick" persons with a set of symbolic habits or induce those so placed to opt for one set of symbolic preferences rather than another. Generalization relating symbolic structure to social structure is likely to be their aim, and their claims will rest on a "correspondence" theory of truth: that their claims accurately (and falsifiably) represent (correspond to) events that actually occur, or are likely to occur, in the empirically palpable world.

Sociology of culture in its "positivist" form (or as *Naturswissenschaft*) is apt to treat pieces of culture as dependent variables and the relevant sectors of social structure as independent variables. This is most commonly seen in standard survey research where, for example, the study of attitudes (conceived as pieces of internalized culture) is designed in such a way that attitudes are simply assumed to be the caused outcome of the demographic structure, the embedded social location of persons, or of the interaction of their several dimensions. Few survey analysts seem upset or disturbed by their apparently puppet-like image of humanity, manipulated by the invisible hand of social structure, which induces attitudes, opinions, or postures toward this and that; no agonizing about "agency" among them. Identifying themselves as social *scientists*, they want to know what correlates with what and the paths that causality treads. Usable determinisms are what they're about.

On the other hand, ethnographers, historical sociologists, and depth interviewers usually have at least some ties to the humanities, to the traditions of *Geisteswissenschaft*, where a manipulated image of human beings is more problematic, less taken for granted, even actively opposed by a view of humankind as free (rationally or not) to choose its own future, of culture as enabling and empowering rather than constraining, of the interaction of social structures as so complex as to defy efforts at simple causal generalization.

Is there a real problem here? I think not. If there appears to be one it is partly an expression of different conceptual aims and partly one of different modes of gathering data. Those who work in a scientific tradition usually seek empirical generalizations. They read general cultural information or use extant theory or their impressions to make formal hypotheses; at their best they gather carefully sampled data from documents, interviews, or observation that, they hope, will test their hypotheses rigorously. They often don't know, or don't know much about, the persons who provide the data beyond what the questionnaire or the primitive demographic information in documents supplies; they are typically less interested in persons than in slices of behavior relevant to their hypotheses. Andrew Greeley, the Roman Catholic priest-novelist-sociologist, is unique in his ability to use formal survey research for the full evocations of persons, although even he must employ different genres to do so. By his own account he uses what he has learned about Catholic Americans from his National Opinion Research Center surveys to create the stories that constitute his best-selling novels—and in a self-sustaining cycle, the royalties from his popular fiction fund further surveys providing the information from which new novels spring.

Those who work in a "humanistic" tradition seek convincing interpretations of lived culture in all its wholeness. Good ethnographers, historical sociologists, and depth interviewers usually work with single (or relatively few) cases, and they may apologize for the absence of rigorous sampling. But they come into possession of very complex data about lived life, ethnographers from being there (and participating) as the life is lived, historians from sometimes obscure and all-but-forgotten primary documents, and depth interviewers from having persons spill out their minds and guts to them.

Possessing data like these is likely to motivate such researchers to render the meanings of social and cultural life in a manner that maximally utilizes the complexity of their data. It is also likely to encourage the casting of a skeptical eye on the superficiality of the kinds of research that seek general causal propositions about the determinate relations among social and symbolic variables.

But where the great strength of research works like *Habits of the Heart* is in the vivid evocation of recognizable persons in all their cultural complexity, acting persons tend to disappear from the work of culturologists when they attempt to get seriously theoretical, and in this respect, ironically, some culturology turns out be not unlike survey research, where persons are seldom vividly present. In syntactical terms, the typical practice of many culturologists, when theorizing, is either (1) to use reified cultural abstractions as the subjects of active or transitive verbs (love conquers all; justice demands that we . . . ; individualism throws new light on . . .) or (2) to use verbs in the passive voice when referring to the dynamics of culture. In either case, acting persons are curiously absent, and who is doing what to whom against what opposition and with what consequences for the collective culture remains *necessarily* obscure. Thus, Marshall Sahlins (1976, 174), semiotically reading the "cultural logic" of food taboos, concludes, "Dogs and horses are thus deemed inedible" (notice the passive voice). A sociologist of culture would want to know *who* deems horses and dogs inedible (and who doesn't—as graduate students my roommates and I ate more than a little horsemeat in the 1950s; it was cheap, lean, and nourishing) and under what conditions and with what consequences for the transmission and modification of that middlingly abstract chunk of culture called "food taboos."

This can be a complex matter. My immigrant father, a moderately observant though far from orthodox Jew, would routinely eat sliced boiled ham or bacon on sandwiches but would become nauseated at the very thought of a pork chop, a roast, or spareribs. Why? A culturological explanation might argue that it's more difficult to conjure an image of the forbidden pig, in all its *treife* (unclean) splendor, from the pink slice of processed meat or the marbled strip of bacon (whose inferential connection to a proscribed living animal is obscure) than from the chop, the ribs, or a roast. A structural/circumstantial explanation might invoke the fact that ham sandwiches and BLTs on toast were routine fare at quick lunch counters during the period of his acculturation, whereas the heavier, dinner-like chops, ribs, or roast loin, visibly "pork," would never be purchased or prepared by his wife for an evening meal at home. The first explanation involves a purely cultural understanding of the problem; an interpretive "reading" of the meat symbolism itself and the psycho-logic it implies. The second involves locating the food taboo in a set of material circumstances invoked in an effort to explain persistence (no ribs, no roast) and change (bacon ok) in food taboos.

Both are necessary because food taboos are not only symbolic but also markers of social identity. "Deep" cultural understanding, achieved through "compelling" interpretation, *and* circumstantial explanation are essential to any serious theoretical effort generalizing relationships between social and symbolic structures. Weber surely understood this clearly. The interpretive conclusions from *The Protestant Ethic and the Spirit of Capitalism* had the logical status of a good (if controversial) hypothesis about the relation of Calvinist Protestantism to western economic development. But he knew that a single "case study" was inadequate to warrant his efforts to generalize about the relation of theologies to economic systems. He needed comparative studies of other religions and other economies in order to do that. Hence, the studies of China, India, and ancient Judaism. It was Weber's genius (and the basis of his lasting reputation) to be able to combine an interpretation of the cultural materials (elements of theological doctrine, the "spirit" of economic enterprise) with an analysis of their circumstantial grounding in the structures of business and religious organizations through his comparative historical studies in which events (if not persons, as is the case with good ethnographies) are vividly evoked in behalf of a theory connecting social structure to symbolic structure. Weber's greatness, in terms of what I have been saying here, resides in his successful merging of culturology with a sociology of culture.

12 / A NOTE ON REDUCTIONISM AND REIFICATION

Everybody knows (or should know) that real life is usually more complex and subtle than the analytic categories and other abstractions that social scientists must use to make generalizations. Weber's "ideal types," for example, have come in for much criticism because their distortions and oversimplifications of empirical reality can be misleading. One response (often associated with "postmodern" sensibilities) has been a kind of superempiricism that regards generalization and theoretic explanation as futile, boring, or otherwise dispensable; that regards each case or research setting as unique, in a strict sense noncomparable to any other, fully explainable by detailed description without "explanation." The research task, then, becomes one of rendering that uniqueness by accounts of closely observed practices in the chunk of culture, sector of society, or set of events under study. That level of scholarly attention to detail surely deserves great praise. Still, some of the purposes of social science are defeated when researchers get so close to "unique" lived experience that they have no generalizable wisdom to pass on to their successors and can only see the complexities to be described and interpreted, rather than the ways in which the data can be *reduced* to parsimonious generalization.

I emphasize "reduced" because the spectre of reductionism is an important subtext of the debates among sociologists interested in the study of culture. Partisans of the effectiveness of "human agency," cultural autonomy, or historical uniqueness are likely to see the structural determinists as guilty of reductionism (by which they seem to mean reducing culture to social structure, hence neglecting agency and oversimplifying human complexity), although the basic impulse of science (if not always its actual practice) *is* reductionist. The determinists, partisans of empirical generalization, are likely to see the partisans of agency as guilty of mystification, although culture *is* deeply and endlessly mysterious.

Freud attempted to understand culture by "reducing" it to a sublimated expression of repressed erotic gratification. Durkheim, on the other hand, opposed efforts to reduce "social facts" to psychological elements. Both formulations may be understood as efforts to pursue interests: material interests because both Freud and Durkheim were leaders of practical efforts to establish autonomous intellectual disciplines (psychoanalysis and sociology) against vigorous and more-than-skeptical opposition from established savants; and ideal interests because the theoretical cogency of their ideological work was a central part of those material efforts. I fancy myself an interpretive humanist *and* a determinist who can afford not to worry about the status of human agency or the autonomy of culture, because, at this time, I have every confidence that their mysteries will long survive the efforts of determinism to reduce them to social structure—which is not a good reason for not *trying* to reduce them.

Even if I were aware that what I say on these pages had been "determined" by material factors or interests, the worthwhileness of saying it would remain because, with so many variables operating, no one is ever *fully* aware of all the specific forces at work. One great virtue of a determinist approach is that it sensitizes us to the external forces at work in our thinking, helps us to focus on them, and, therefore, by a reflexive process, deepens whatever obscure "autonomy" may in fact be there. This, it seems to me, is precisely the educational, even liberational, function of determinism: by threatening the perhaps *falsely* autonomous character of thinking it forces us back into the received sources of thought, where we may (or may not) find more authentic autonomies. Assertions about the (even if limited) freedoms of human agency, the autonomy of culture, and the uniqueness of events ought to be tested in the acids of a determinist perspective. What survives that test will then surely deserve a respect that is more than sentimental.

A lot of the literature in the sociology of culture uses terms like "reductionism," "deterministic," and "reification" in an almost exclusively pejorative way (see Wuthnow et al. 1984 for an extreme example; there are many others). I myself have sometimes thoughtlessly fallen into such usage. It seems to me, however, that any intellectual work that claims even roughly to belong in a scientific tradition *must* be conducted in a determinist spirit; it wants to know what causes what. It must also be reductionistic if it wants to wrest some relatively simple generalization from the infinitely complex data of lived life. That's why we need abstract concepts, and why we study the empirical relations among them or their indicators. But all abstractions are simplifications, and they all have a tendency to become reifications when scholars deploy them, in argument, as nouns, in sentences, and especially in sentences where they become the subjects of transitive verbs. And if you know what you're doing it is not necessarily misleading to speak as if abstractions *acted* with consequence in the real world. Mary Douglas's most recent book was titled *How Institutions Think*, and she makes a good Durkheimian case that they do—"good," in part, because she does so without in any way threatening Weber's nominalism (or methodological individualism). It is surely useful and important to know *who*, specifically, is acting, particularly in ways that sustain the vitality and validity of the abstractions. But sometimes social scientists don't know or can't afford to stop and find out, and hence invoke usage such as "society says," "tradition dictates that we," or, roughly paraphrasing myself, "abstractions have a tendency to . . ." So when we feel critical of reductionisms, determinisms, and reifications, it's not these intellectual processes *in general* we're legitimately critical of, but the specific ways in which, and purposes for which, they have been deployed. It is a question of ideology being avowed or disavowed.

✳

2

Research in the
Sociology of Culture

13 / IDEOLOGICAL WORK IN EMPIRICAL STUDIES OF CULTURE

Not long ago Jeffrey Alexander said that the major issue in contemporary sociological theory was to reintegrate subjective voluntarism and objective constraint. I hope in this essay to make a "contribution" to the reintegration, but I want to do that not by engaging contemporary theorists in one more endless debate but by examining critically a variety of relatively recent *empirical* works in the sociology of culture. Like the questions of general (or Grand) theorizing that concern Alexander, the central issue that divides scholars in the sociology of culture (at least in the French and English speaking countries) may also be seen as an issue of voluntarism versus determinism (sometimes also designated as the question of choice vs. constraint, or the claims of individual agency vs. those of social structure). But the issue of choice versus constraint has been clouded by the different modes of research in which the issue gets posed. Voluntarism is most often found in the modes of research one can label "humanist" or *Geisteswissenschaften;* structuralist determinism is most often found in the modes of research designed on the model of *Naturswissenschaften.* But the correlation is far from perfect, and there are lots of mixed or "blurred" genres, which is why the issue is often clouded. At its extremes, however, it seems clear, for example, that for survey researchers voluntarism is hardly an issue; they simply assume that the sampled attitudes they study are structurally dependent variables "caused," determined, or influenced to one extent or another by the independent variables they try to control. At the other extreme, field ethnographers and depth interviewers get to know so much about the relatively few people (or cases) they study that it becomes difficult, even reckless, to begin imputing impersonal causalities to the complex culture revealed to them by the persons they directly confront in research. Between these extremes, though, the research genres become less purely "humanist" or "positivist," and it takes close scrutiny to perceive the character of the interplay between choice and structural constraint.

The "claims of social structure" here refers not to the "structuralism" of Lévi-Strauss or Althusser but to the general sociological orientation that looks to social structures as the major source for understanding the cultural categories and rhetorics by which individual and group actions are legitimated. An emphasis on "agency," on the other hand, is simply current code for resisting the view that felt culture may be adequately understood by studying its external causes, and for affirming subjective choice as at least to some extent internally generated or free of determination. Can culture be "reduced" to social structure? Can it be adequately understood purely as a dependent variable, even when the actions of persons that reveal and "carry" culture are felt by them as willed and chosen from alternatives? Or is culture autonomous—or, like the state, "relatively autonomous"? If so, relative to what and for how long?

I will come back to these questions toward the end of this essay. For now, however, more important than the divisions is the fact that a distinctive sociology of culture has taken shape in Western countries—even in the U.S. where, in 1986, a small group of sociologists succeeded in officially establishing a section on the sociology of culture within the American Sociological Association, and in less than a year accumulated a dues-paying membership of nearly four hundred persons. In some respects, the sociology of culture is much like other specialized subfields of sociology, having a distinctive subject matter (symbols/meanings). In other respects, though, it is unlike most other specialized sociological fields because in the modern world, culture has acquired a quasi-sacred character (particularly for those indifferent to religion), and a sociology of it sometimes teeters at the edge of sacrilege. All sociological orientations that try to discover the social causes of individual behavior invite resistance from those made morally uneasy by it, offensive as it is to their sense of individual freedom and choice. A sociological orientation to culture is also "counterintuitive" because, of all felt experience, conscious beliefs are most likely to feel like "one's own," a part of one's very being. An effort to understand those beliefs as externally caused rather than internally chosen, therefore, can feel very much like an expropriation, an explaining-away rather than an explanation.

Sociology of culture invites especially stiff resistance owing also, I think, to the "noble" character of some of its distinctive subject matter. Dealing as culture does with art, science, religion, values, and taste, few people are likely to want to hear that the nature and character of their conceptions of truth, beauty, or goodness might have "reasons" or causes other than (or in addition to) what they think they are—particularly when the most prominent and self-conscious seekers after that trinity of values are predominantly intellectuals, who are (and must be—why else would they do intellectual work?) among the most vain about the autonomy of their symbolic efforts.

In his introduction to the English edition of Karl Mannheim's *Ideology and Utopia*, Louis Wirth made the often quoted assertion that every statement of fact about the social world touches the interests of some group. It seems equally probable that every sociological statement about culture touches the quasi-sacred interests of some group. To study culture sociologically is to walk on eggs, and to study the culture of intellectuals (i.e., those who study culture and discuss it) is to walk on eggs with especially brittle shells.

I want here to provide specific examples of this problem by describing several instances of fairly recent research in the sociology of culture, and then commenting on how each researcher has attempted to cope interpretively with some of the ideological difficulties generated by the findings themselves. Some readers may infer derogatory intentions in my effort to focus on the *situation* of the researchers, and on the ways in which those situations affect the researchers' modes of ideologically coping with the data; far from it. I have selected for analysis very good work (I recommended the publication of three of the books under consideration), and my efforts to extract the ideologies operating in them are meant to show how appeals to the criteria and conventions (some sturdy, some less so) of the warranting communities that sanction a piece of research as "good work" inevitably enter into even the best sociology. That ideological work is done in the research to be considered here, then, does not necessarily (although it may, and occasionally does) indicate flaws or weaknesses in the work. The question is where and how the ideology gets into the empirical work, and how subtle or sophisticated the ideological work is. Like any other profession, sociology is situated in what Bourdieu calls a "field" with its own more or less strongly sanctioned conventions, and its practitioners occupy positions in that field to which they bring personal histories that shape the ways in which they exercise the prerogatives and cope with the constraints of that position. I hope to show some of this at work in each case specifically.

I have some more abstract aims as well. As I said, one of them is to help reintegrate structuralism and voluntarism. One of the typical occasions for ideological work in sociological research occurs when authors must face the question of the extent to which their findings indicate the operation of impersonal determining forces and/or the willed choices by the people who provide the data. The data themselves are often not conclusive in this respect. But the issue will not go away, and in dealing with it authors may then indulge their predispositions toward voluntarism or determinism.

Another aim—and a part of the strategy of reintegration—is to restore some dignity to the word "ideology," which ought to describe efforts to legitimate a controversial argument, policy, or developing course of action (instead of referring simply to suspect or deceptive arguments). These efforts, almost always partly improvised owing to the unavoidable contingencies of the situations in which they occur, may be brilliant or clumsy (or anywhere between), but they are necessary (and therefore always important) where the legitimations are not a self-evident part of an accepted culture—increasingly the case in plural and diverse societies where contentiousness over culture is prevalent, and in sociology itself where paradigm conflict is routine.

First, I will take up some predominantly "structuralist" works, beginning with my own:

1. In my field research on counterculture communes in rural California I developed the concept of "ideological work"—in part to describe the efforts of communards to cope intellectually with discrepancies, discontinuities, and apparent contradictions between the beliefs that they brought to communal life and the constraints of actually living with those beliefs in a communal environment. But I also used "ideological work" to defend myself (and, by extension, any ethnographer so situated) against the passion with which my communards were telling me what they believed as persuasively as they could. When people talk passionately about what they believe regarding matters on which several beliefs are possible, plausible, available, and accessible, sociological interpretation is invited by that fact, and it seemed to me that I could not thoroughly understand the meanings of what they were telling me unless I could relate those beliefs to the structure of the specific circumstances in which the believers were more or less stuck (that cognitive tactic, of course, helped me defend myself against their passion). Although "more or less" is an important qualifier, "stuck" is the operative term here because it is seldom easy to change one's basic social situation. It is usually less difficult to alter or modify one's beliefs (probably imperceptibly or gradually but sometimes quite suddenly or abruptly) so that they seem more reasonable, prudent, or realistic (or otherwise persuasive) given the limits and possibilities of one's position.

The seed of the concept of ideological work was probably planted in me quite young. One of the earliest postwar plays and films about the drug problem was called *A Hatful of Rain* (film 1957). The plot pivots on the discovery by a stern father that his son, an apparent model of rectitude, is addicted to heroin. Before the discovery, the father is characterized as a severe disciplinarian, a paragon of the Protestant ethic, and proud of his son. But when the evidence of his son's addiction is presented, he does not turn on his son in a rage of betrayal; instead, recovering from the initial shock of the discovery, he says with a defensive shrug, "Well, everybody takes a little something," the father's moral severity thus yielding a bit to his love for his son in circumstances he could neither control nor alter.

We might call this, with some contempt, a case of "rationalization." But as I thought more about it, what we call rationalization seemed to me only a particularly clumsy, transparent, or primitive form of ideological work. Good ideological work is not often perceived as rationalization though it is surely intended to rationalize, that is, to make reasonable, persuasive or defensible. By the term "ideological work," then, I intended to refer to efforts to legitimate (or delegitimate) decisions, actions, and events, especially under conditions where some opposition to (or support for) them could be anticipated and to reconcile or alter those efforts as apparent inconsistencies or contradictions were revealed among them and as material conditions changed in ways that affected the viability or persuasiveness of those efforts. The limiting case, of course, is ideological rigidity—what we call either fanaticism or devotion to principle, depending usually on whether we approve or disapprove of the particular principle or behavior in question.

Given that situation, the analytic task is to see how those beliefs do or do not "work" to legitimate the actions and policies proceeding from that situation (i.e., whether the ideological work is effective) and to confer some honor or dignity on the actors who formulate and adhere to them. The simplest example from the commune research is this: according to long-standing ideas about child rearing in the U.S., children require close supervision by parents, a long period of socialization (late maturity), and great inputs of time, money, and energy. Communards did not have the requisite resources to sustain such child-rearing practices, being both very poor and very busy with the heavy physical and emotional tasks of creating and sustaining the rural settlement—even if they initially believed in the dominant ideas, which they did not. I found it unsurprising that they on the whole rejected dominant child-rearing ideas; any effort to live up to those ideas would almost certainly have failed. Instead, they favored "alternative" ideas about child rearing, ideas that their situation and their resources enabled them to live up to and feel good about. Their image of children was rather romantic if not Rousseauian: a little sun, water, food, breathing space, and like healthy plants children grow up straight, tall, and vigorous—and mature early to take on adult rights and responsibilities. Here we have some ideas about children that imply a kind of benign neglect as wholesome—suggesting that children are less in need of intense "raising" than of safe and nourishing spaces in which they can thrive on their own, with the help of adults always available should the children require it.

The ideological work consists of a mélange of moral and empirical or logical argument designed to legitimate their course of action regarding children and to confer honor on those who undertake it. It is, of course, also used against those predisposed to be critical of it ("child-neglect," etc.) and to delegitimate their arguments by invoking, for example, images of excessive parental pressure on middle class boys, motherly smothering, invidious gender socialization, juvenilization, and so on. Ideological work is always necessary where culture has lost its hegemonic character, and where, therefore, cultural pluralism, even if not prevalent, is at least a potentiality that exposes extant legitimacies to criticism and argument.

Child rearing is an especially good example because, as I suggested earlier, in terms of the criteria of routine science we reliably "know" rather little about the relation between how parents raise children and the developmental outcomes of their work. Yet most parents will find it intolerable to accept the fact that much of the time they don't really know what they are doing. They (we) therefore need expertly sanctioned ideas about child rearing, which, however, reliably tell them less about children than about the needs of parents for coherence and authority in their management of children. At this writing there is a continuing controversy over the dinosaur violence in the film *Jurassic Park* and whether it is safe for children of a certain age to see it. Surely this has less to do with the probable nightmares of children—about which we reliably know little—than with the increasing constraints on middle-class parents to shelter and protect their children from the brutalities of the world. My own childhood was filled with Dracula and Frankenstein and Zombies and King Kong (in which dinosaurs eat people whole). Did I have nightmares? I certainly did; all children—and adults—do, though I don't remember any of them being about movie characters. These days "the culture says" good parents must protect their children from ugly prospects and realities, which is why we buy Volvos, move out of "bad" neighborhoods, rate movies, and censor TV.

But it was not only the communards who had to do ideological work; I had to do it also, if only to defend myself against the passion of their arguments. Several times during the period of field research I found it necessary to remove myself physically from a rural commune in order to consider "objectively" (i.e., in more familiar, more comfortable, and less threatening surroundings—objectivity itself requires certain material conditions for its proper exercise) what they were passionately trying to persuade me of. In fact, the very concept of ideological work, which looks for the meanings of beliefs in the social situation of those who believe them, functioned as an ideology for me, lending legitimacy to my detachment and honoring my identity as a social scientist studying the meanings of culture.

Still, analytic detachment, if one thinks about it for a moment in a detached way, is a truly bizarre ideology except in a few highly professionalized contexts. The kinds of assertions one finds, for example, in journalism and social science about the propriety of objectivity are actually applied primarily when one's work involves or implies judgments likely to generate public controversy. Where values are deeply consensual or taken for granted, professionals in journalism or social science usually don't hesitate to give some moral edge or tone to the facts; the costs of doing that are likely to be minimal or nil. Note the wrinkled-brow sympathetic piety on the faces of newscasters reporting child-abuse or abductions; note the predictably sympathetic ethnographies of the aged, the poor, the homeless, or other groups with respect to whom widespread public sympathy is assumed. (Sports journalists, oddly, seem utterly exempt from the distinctions between news, opinion, and editorializing.) And in the hard sciences, you don't find cancer or AIDS researchers, for example, going on at great length about how careful they've been to separate facts and values. That separation is an assumed part of the culture of science, except perhaps when researchers seek funding. Besides, their audiences *want* to be reminded that researchers trying to find cures for fatal diseases are embarked on a noble crusade. But if the facts are in any way controversial in their moral/political implications (particularly, as Dan Hallin [1986] has pointed out, if they are likely to divide elites), then a professional objective posture is typically taken, which (as Alvin Gouldner [1970] concluded in his study of Auguste Comte's role in the history of sociology) functions as a defensive or protective device for the investigator; protection against seduction or "going native" and against "interests" that may be offended by "biased" conclusions.

But detached professionals are likely to have their morally righteous buttons pushed most effectively when *professional* pieties are breached, rather than general moral pieties. A person may be a sonofabitch in all his interpersonal relations, and colleagues will reserve judgment. But if he breaches "professional ethics" (lawyers sleeping with clients, doctors with patients, professors with students, etc.) collegial scorn is likely to be heaped upon him. Why? Because violation of professional norms directly threatens the material interests of the whole group, while more routine or banal forms of bad behavior or cruelty do not.

2. In *Abortion and the Politics of Motherhood* my former California colleague Kristin Luker reports on a study of the women leaders of the "pro-choice" and "pro-life" movements. Professor Luker is a well-known feminist and she is also a very good and perceptive sociologist, and in her interviews with the leaders of the anti-abortion groups she

found herself increasingly moved by the depth and sincerity of what these leaders told her. During the period of her research she would occasionally come by my office (down the corridor from hers) to express her concern about being emotionally captured by an ideology she had intellectually rejected. Why? Because her research was showing that there were large and systematic social differences between the two groups of women: pro-choice leaders had far more education and family income, fewer children, and more frequent (often professional) employment outside the home than pro-life leaders. From the point of view, therefore, of a woman lawyer earning perhaps $100,000 a year, with a husband of similar earning capacity, and, say, one or two children cared for by a full-time nanny they can afford, an unexpected pregnancy can be a major threat to her career and style of life. But for a woman with little education, few salable skills, and perhaps three or four children, all of them exclusively dependent on her husband's income, an unexpected pregnancy is not only not a threat to her career; in a sense it *is* her career. Looked at this way, the abortion controversy turns out to be less a purely moral, philosophical or religious (i.e., "cultural") problem than a problem that taps at least some of its intensity from the material interests of women situated in systematically different ways in the social structure.

Among other things, Luker learned from her research that where conflicting ideologies each have their own plausible moral logic (as in the abortion controversy), which one is found to be persuasive or convincing depends in some large part upon one's social placement and the structure of resources (in Bourdieu's terms, the social or cultural capital) to be found there. But it also showed her that, given the situation of many pro-life women, their ideology made sense for them because motherhood and homemaking were (either explicitly or in effect) being proclaimed as the noblest career for women. Luker, of course, is a woman with a lot of education, a very good income, and a prestigious career, but she is also an academic scholar. Therefore an empirical and objective posture was a far better solution to what, for her, was a very personal problem; better, that is, than the overtly feminist posture she adopted in her first book, *Taking Chances* (on contraception), written when she was still a graduate student. She was objective in seeing that it was difficult to understand the moral intensity of ideologies about abortion without understanding their implications in the social structure of women's careers and the politics of motherhood. And she was empirically predictive (rather than morally hortatory) in expecting that as higher education becomes increasingly available to women (and as they, therefore, become increasingly present in the well-paid labor force) fewer women will find it necessary to depend solely on motherhood, homemaking, and husbands as their major sources of honor. Her book was widely praised for its balance, compassion, and moderation. Even some anti-abortionists were sympathetic to the book, perhaps because they expected a contentious tract from a well-known feminist. But the book received some hostile reviews from feminists who regarded Luker's balanced analysis as a betrayal of her feminist loyalties. Her ideological work consists in having made a case for the "rationality" of the pro-life argument without giving up her support for pro-choice, and good ideological work it is.

3. Paul Willis's *Learning to Labor* has had important influences in his native United Kindgdom and in the United States. Yet it has also been influential in France, perhaps because it cites Pierre Bourdieu more than once but also because it demonstrates ethnographically the interpenetration of structure and agency that Bourdieu outlines so persuasively in theoretical terms but cannot demonstrate persuasively with the survey data he typically relies on. What Bourdieu tells us abstractly about the influences of "habitus" on agency Willis shows us empirically. He takes a group of English working-class boys of fifteen, in their last year of school before entering the unskilled labor force, and he shows us how the system of social stratification is reproduced by the motivated choices (i.e., "agency") of these boys to find fun and satisfaction in exactly the kinds of behavior that preclude their doing well in school, and

hence guarantee the reproduction of the class system. They smoke, drink, get sex, and carouse; they are truant and generally disobedient and disrespectful to school authorities. As they put it, they "have a laff."

Willis finds much of this rather touching, even poignant, and there is some evidence that he himself identifies with these boys, perhaps having come from a similar background and certainly being one who achieved considerable upward mobility. The poignance of his portrayal comes not only from his (vicarious?) identification with "the lads" but also from his stated conviction that their anti-school ideology (which he details at some length) is "rational"—not unlike the ways in which the child-rearing ideology of communards and the pro-life and pro-choice ideologies make sense for those structurally situated groups who espouse them. Obeying the school's rules and otherwise being "good boys" are not likely to have much payoff for them. The school, after all, does not control the labor market, and their conformity to the rules will not necessarily get them much better jobs. In the meantime they seem to have more fun than the "good" boys, who will also graduate to seek places in the unskilled labor market, and probably not do much better. It is a bleak portrayal in the sense that Bourdieu's is bleak in both *Reproduction* and *Distinction*. But there is also a difference. Bourdieu uses survey data, and he does not know his respondents personally. Willis is an ethnographer, and he not only knows his boys but he likes them as well. They see through ("penetrate") the self-serving ideology of the school and he admires them for that—although they do not see through it clearly enough to do anything to improve their situation.

Unlike Luker or myself, Willis writes as a committed socialist throughout his book. His discourse is objective, but it is not detached. His reference group is clearly the British Left, and his discourse is explicitly both sociological and political. As a left-sociologist participating in neo-Marxist debate, he wants to argue that working-class culture is not simply a mechanical reflection of the constraints of class placement, not simply a case of "false consciousness" imposed by a ruling class intent on perpetuating its domination. Whether Willis's experience of working-class culture was vicarious or authentic, he wants to honor that experience by rendering it as vividly and as vitally as he can, and his ideological work consists in that effort to bring his boys alive as conscious agents. In Willis's eyes, they *choose* their anti-school ideology and they are authentically motivated by it—although their choices, as Willis reminds us again and again, are from a very limited range of structured possibilities. As a partisan of the working class, Willis wants to impress on us the authenticity of its lived culture; as a neo-Marxist, he cannot evade the fact that what is authentically chosen is selected from so constricted a range of possibility as to render the very idea of choice ironic. The most poignant dilemma of Willis's book is his romantic reluctance to yield his admiration for the lads' resistance, despite his own convincing evidence of its counterproductiveness.

In the American edition of *Learning to Labor* there is an appendix in which Willis replies to those critics of the first edition of the book who complained that his sympathy for "the lads" was misplaced since they are explicitly racist, sexist, and sometimes behave much like thugs. There is no need here to cite the details of his response but only to observe—again—that we find an author constrained to do ideological work *about his own findings* and interpretations—in this instance to protect his credentials as a man of the democratic Left.

4. Robert Jackson has published the results of his purely historical-structural study of the relationship between capitalism and gender inequality. He finds direct correlations between the bureaucratization of capitalist enterprise and the decline of gender inequality (operationalized by a variety of specific measures). His interpretation is basically that the logic of rationalization (in Weber's sense) discourages discriminations of this sort and hence reduces (though of course does not eliminate) inequality between the sexes. Some of these findings and interpretations, initially reported in an oral colloquium, made feminists in the audience rather angry. They inferred from Jackson's analysis that he regarded feminist ideology and consciousness-raising as having played

little or no role in the reduction of inequality, and their criticism of his work was vigorous. But Jackson had apparently heard this criticism before and he was ready for it. His research, he said, used a logic of historical correlation; it said little or nothing about the actual psychological or interpersonal processes through which the correlations were worked out—presumably by motivated "agents" making choices. Feminist militance *may* have played an important part (in conjunction with bureaucratic rationalization), but if such is the case it required asking different questions and using different methods and research designs in order to answer them. I call that reasonably effective ideological work, especially in its strategy of pleading ignorance and shifting the burden of proof to those who would argue for the efficacy of consciousness-raising. Jackson's strategy rather reminds me of the apocryphal Kinsey Institute sex researcher replying to a woman who complained that the Kinsey research ignored the role of love in sexual behavior: "Look, lady, you want to study love? Go study love. We study sex."

But this little contretemps between Jackson and his feminist critics reveals also some more general ideological disputes among social scientists regarding modes and methods of research. Survey researchers and historical/comparative scholars who deal with large and abstract units of analysis (nations, institutional systems, classes, etc.) often know little or nothing about how the patterns or regularities they discover are actually accomplished or established through the culture-rich and culture-pervasive interpersonal processes that ultimately constitute them. Because they don't know much about how their findings are produced at the level of interpersonal relations, macro-sociologists (and their readers) remain pretty much in the dark about how stable or reliable those regularities are likely to be over time. Attention to interpersonal processes, of course, constitutes the strength of the micro-sociologies of field ethnographers and depth interviewers; at their best they provide us with evidence of the lived experience of those stuck in the structures that macro-sociologists describe, and, by showing us how people deal with that stuckness, can provide some insight into how stable those structures are likely to be over time; where the culturally reproductive forces are strong and where they face incipient resistance and are hence vulnerable to change.

But like macro-sociologies, many of which are forgotten or become obsolete only a few years after they are completed, micro-sociologies too are not always at their best. Who needs one more ethnographic case study? What do twenty-five non-random depth interviews prove? Hostile questions such as these are often asked by large-sample survey researchers interested in generalization and hypothesis-testing, and by document-using macro-sociologists whose interest in understanding large institutional events predisposes them to see most micro-interactional studies as trivial—except perhaps in the hands of acknowledged brilliance, like Erving Goffman's.

The hostile questions are not without point: perhaps there isn't much need for another ethnography confirming in a specific case the already conventional wisdom, and a case study, like a handful of interviews, does not conclusively "prove" anything general. But by focusing on how macro-regularities are experienced by living persons and on how macro-cultural constraints are interpreted (and otherwise coped with) in specific situations, micro sociologies give us the rare (in social science) opportunity to know something about how socially located persons struggle with "conditions" that, in Marx's terms, they did not entirely choose, struggles that, even when defeated by conspiracies of circumstance and "agency" (as with Willis's "lads"), show them not going gently into that good night.

These constitute the lasting strengths of sociology's "classic" ethnographies like *Street Corner Society, All Our Kin,* and *Talley's Corner.* It is perhaps for reasons like this that vivid ethnographies and revealing reports of depth interviews often gather a wide variety of readers—including those who are not social scientists; readers recognize a little of themselves in the persons so portrayed. It's a bit more difficult to see oneself in a "dependent variable" or in an abstraction called "bureacratization" or "gender inequality." This, of course, is far from the last word on macro- versus micro-sociologies. But it does indicate some of the latent (and unresolved) ideological disputes among professionals behind Jackson's defensiveness about his own findings and regarding the feminist criticism of them.

5. Chandra Mukerji has conducted research on the funding by the U.S. government of basic scientific research in the deep oceans. She raises the question of why government funds this very expensive research that may have no short-run applied or practical use, and of how scientists go about trying to persuade government to continue funding them. Her book is titled *A Fragile Power* because it is concerned with the extent to which scientists can protect and sustain their autonomy (relative autonomy?) when their large networks of laboratories and thousands of employees are dependent on funding decisions of the National Science Foundation, the U.S. Navy, and other government agencies. She shows us elite scientists whose combined roles as funding entrepreneurs, academic politicians, and seekers after new knowledge are inextricably mixed. She shows us the delicate negotiations conducted between senior scientists interested in maintaining their expensive research establishments and government administrators of funds who must make decisions, sometimes on the basis of conflicting advice from other senior scientists and competing research establishments. She shows us ocean scientists fumbling around in their deep ocean research vehicles trying to determine what it *is* that they are seeing down there (some of it has never been seen before), often in language most unscientific. They take Walter Cronkite (the then CBS newscaster and "most trusted man in America") along for the favorable publicity he can provide.

In addition to its empirical merits, the work is conceptually inventive. Among the virtues of close-up interviewing and observation are the fresh concepts that sometimes emerge from them (e.g., relative deprivation, civil inattention, reference groups, ideological work). In this case Mukerji designates soft-money scientists an "elite reserve labor force," and here the ideological problems begin. The reserve labor force idea has been used before, of course, but it has been used primarily to describe that 5 to 10 percent of the mostly unskilled labor supply who at any given moment are unemployed, and whom welfare states support until labor shortages require their services. The idea of an *elite* reserve labor force comes out of her analysis of the balancing of tensions between the different interests of science and government. Elite scientists want to do basic research and maintain their labs. Government, though it may not have much interest in pure research without short-run applied significance, does have interests in maintaining and sharpening the research skills of elite scientists *in case* they should be needed in national emergencies like war, epidemic disease, or ecological or economic crisis. Moreover, scientists know this, and know they have the power to lend their skills elsewhere, ultimately, for example, by emigration, and they use this knowledge (in Bourdieu's terms "cultural capital") as the negotiations proceed.

But the elite reserve labor force idea is ideologically edgy (the walking-on-eggs problem again) because it suggests a structural parallelism between a lumpen proletariat and elite scientists. That implies a sort of status degradation for scientists, and the dense mixture of basic research with politics and fund-raising threatens to impugn the public image of science as "pure."

The ideological implications get still more complex. In writing a book about such ideologically sensitive matters, Mukerji, like Luker and Jackson, adopts the conventional academic posture of detachment. Her prose is cool, descriptive, objective; her style is almost toneless, without edge. Ironically, the first draft of the book was criticized for exactly its neutral rhetoric on the grounds that such *interesting* findings deserve a more flamboyant style of presentation, if only to ensure that they get *noticed*. Here, obviously, is a problem of audience. Sometimes audiences are ready-made, either because the author is already famous or the subject matter is of broad public interest or central to an established field of academic study. But if none of these conditions is present, authors, in order to *find* an audience not already there and waiting, must sometimes do the ideological work necessary for an audience to "hear" what is being said, and to find it interesting and credible. Some authors have mixed audiences, conflicting or even marginal ones. Mukerji resisted the advice on flamboyance, and though her work was not ignored (indeed, it won an academic prize) its different audiences (historians, sociologists, oceanographers) responded to it in almost predictably different ways. Like other writers, scientists hard and soft must make essentially ideological choices about how most effectively to present their research so that it will not be ignored. There is no reason to believe that these choices are random, as is plainly indicated by the way in which the cold fusion researchers chose to present their results to the world, and by the consequences that followed it.

6. Pierre Bourdieu is perhaps the most sophisticated and elegant sociological writer coping with the problem of saying things about culture that few people want to hear. *Homo Academicus*, for example, is in part concerned with the determinate effects of structural constraints on those guardians of culture, like established academic intellectuals, who are likely to be most sensitive about the autonomy of their thought and action. *Distinction*, on the other hand, purports to be an ethnography of French taste, based largely on survey data. Bourdieu respects quantitative data but he is no positivist. Trained to think epistemologically, he distances himself from the numbers. He knows that the neutral-seeming numbers may contain hidden ideologies. He knows, for example, that the meaning of what people say in reply to questionnaires is seldom self-evident; he knows that a solicited opinion or attitude is one that may not have existed previously, and is hence a reified artifact of the question or interview situation; he knows that the determining property of an independent variable and the determined property of a dependent variable are often mysterious or ambiguous; he knows that questions about the meanings of survey data are often begged by the commonsensical assumptions underlying the codes that classify such

data. Bourdieu seldom falls into the narrative bog of trying to make readable prose out of distributive statistics, but his text is actually less concerned with citing data (which, in any case, contain few surprises for specialists in the sociology of culture) than with using them in behalf of an argument about the relationship of class and status.

Where Weber contrasted the realm of class (life chances in economic markets) and the realm of status (quantum of honor embedded in a style of life), Bourdieu's entire oeuvre—but especially *Distinction*—is an effort to link the two realms by conceiving both as markets that, although moved by different kinds of currency, overlap enough to make their currencies strategically exchangeable. The currency deployable in status markets is "cultural capital." By this term Bourdieu means to distinguish between the power exercised by money (economic capital) and the power exercised by resources inherited or acquired chiefly from family and educational systems: credentials, names, titles; carriage, bearing, voice; linguistic competence, erudition, grace, savoir faire—in short all the skills and facilities that function as assets (and liabilities in some contexts) in the cultural performances of everyday life. Possessors of these assets may deploy them, like economic capital, in markets: displaying, flaunting, investing, threatening, trading or otherwise using them to maintain or enhance a position in the order of class domination. Bourdieu is interested in how such symbolic goods reinforce the advantages of those with sufficient amounts of capital (or the right mix of the different kinds of capital) to control access to markets, the terms of trade, and the value of currency.

The dominant culture of art is rooted in Kantian aesthetics, which defines beauty in terms of the *formal* (not the substantive, moral, or utilitarian) aspects of the aesthetic object, and "good taste" in terms of the cultivated abilities to distinguish mere sensory gratification or enjoyment from reflective pleasure—hence, the coarse from the fine, the facile from the difficult, the mendacious from the disinterested, the common from the rare, the indulgent from the restrained, the banal from the distinguished, and so on through the polarities used by the dominant classes to stigmatize the taste and style of those lower in the order of domination and to dignify the "purity" of their own. These antinomies underlie the specific patterns of preference and practice that on the whole characterize the stratified styles of life evident in the survey data, and which, despite the many differences between French and American culture, are not strikingly different from Herbert Gans's description of the relations between "taste cultures" and social class in the U.S.

The walking-on-eggs problem again: notice here that Bourdieu is consciously desacralizing culture, and he says explicitly that the very discussion of culture's worldly role is itself widely regarded by elites as a vulgarizing if not barbarous exercise for which few will have good reason to be grateful to him. Mary Douglas cites Nancy Mitford as having said that to write a book on taste is itself in bad taste, and Bourdieu is mindful of that constraint. He is, after all, telling us in effect that our deepest and most authentically experienced convictions of affirmation and revulsion, our visceral senses of the true, the beautiful, the good, the natural, the self-evident, in which reside our very sense of who we are, are only (but not at all merely) expressions of the peculiar mix of invested cultural and economic capital that defines our membership in classes, class fractions, and status groups, and our commitments to their associated styles of life.

But in anticipating that elites will be reluctant to "hear" his conclusions about the role of culture in class domination, Bourdieu inadvertently reveals that he is addressing himself primarily to them—not to the dominated classes, whose spokespersons, at least in the U.S., would be delighted to hear the news. The fact that he addresses himself primarily to academic elites, however, governs his ideological strategy in coping with his own findings about the thoroughly social character of "agency," and with the opposition he expects those findings to engender. Unlike Edward Said—or even Foucault (also notably interested in the role of culture in political domination)—Bourdieu is no militant. He has a proper academic's disdain of those who might fault him for the political quiescence perhaps latent in his understanding of the all-but-irresistible role played by high culture in reproducing class domination. His scholar's ideology is severe, ascetic, Weberian, stoic, aloof. On more than one occasion he has expressed something close to contempt for the kinds of academic intellectuals who seek "popular" success; he wants to maintain a clear and unblinking gaze at the truths of power, uncorrupted by sentiment or wishfulness. Despite his desacralization, then, this posture identifies him as a member in good standing of an ascetic elite, and reassures his peers that he is no mere malcontent with a disposition to pander. That's very good ideological work.

Bourdieu also reassures his elite academic audience by not excluding himself from his own generalizations. He is a sufficiently reflexive and skeptical writer that he can usually stay a step or two ahead of his critics. Bourdieu deals with Mannheim's dilemma with a radical skepticism and reflexivity that, as a psychological device, was simply not available to Mannheim in the intellectual culture of his day. The persistent reflexiveness of Bourdieu's style is a continual reminder to his readers that he is subject to the same relations between position, disposition, and predisposition as anyone else. It is also an invitation to his critics to find any distortions engendered by those relations. He almost always anticipates antagonism to the inevitable oversimplifications of general assertion; he often seems to be saying "do not understand me too quickly." He often writes defensively, as if his invisible critics were standing at his shoulder, and he is answering their questions almost before they have been asked. Bourdieu, a virtuoso of reflexivity, at the same time expresses his distrust of it as individualistic showiness.

In addition, *Distinction* wraps its findings and its critique of "legitimate" culture in the most elegant and symbolically rich theoretical package. In part, Bourdieu's originality consists of his having absorbed most of the influential sociological theorists without having become a partisan of any. He is Durkheimian without Durkheim's mystifying reification. Like Parsons, he is relentlessly systematic and more than occasionally opaque—while somehow maintaining an image of himself as an *homme de gauche*. From Lévi-Strauss and the structuralists he has borrowed an eye for the binary character of basic and recurrent cultural motifs; but from Marx he has adopted the insistence that such motifs have a material basis in (and material consequences for) class relations—although he lacks any trace of Marxist activism. He is clearly on familiar terms with Veblen's pecuniary emulation, conspicuous waste, and the endlessness of sought prestige, although there's no mention of Veblen in *Distinction*. From critical theory he has taken his subject matter (the relation of culture to power) but he has discarded the Frankfurt School's preachiness, its search for "objective" values, and its fondness for the "early" (less materialist) Marx. The entire text of *Distinction* can be read as a dialogue with Weber (though he is hardly mentioned), and as an extended footnote to Weber's insight that status is "usurped." Bourdieu's analytic style is reminiscent of his friend Erving Goffman's approach to strategic micro-interaction, except that Bourdieu applies it to macro-cultural issues. In short, this demonstration of his learnedness also demonstrates that he has paid his intellectual dues, which helps to make his disenchanting message more "hearable."

Because the findings of *Distinction* for France are so close to those of Herbert Gans's *Popular Culture and High Culture* for the U.S. it may be instructive to ask why Bourdieu's book won attention and respect from the intellectuals of Europe and the U.S., whereas Gans's book was subject to charges of barbarism from some of the New York intellectuals. How do the two books differ? Gans's style is plain, Bourdieu's elegant; Gans offers plans and policies for greater democratic support of cultural diversity, Bourdieu is apparently *au-dessus de la mêlée*—although not entirely, for, as he says, there is no way out of the culture "game." Most important, Gans is practical, Bourdieu theoretical, and in academic disciplines (even the most empirical ones) the highest prestige is generally given to theorists. Bourdieu offers some comfort to the Left by unmasking the "purity" of high culture but he does not offer much hope that anything important can be changed. His message seems democratic but it is delivered in an impeccably aristocratic envelope—so that it will be opened and read and "heard" as legitimate by academic elites. Bourdieu is even daring enough to remind his readers from time to time that he is doing exactly that—as usual, one step ahead of his critics.

Here is a case of brilliant ideological work, and of a "very French" sort. Whereas in the U.S. an academic scholar can acquire the most prestigious reputation without venturing beyond the boundaries of the specialized journals in his or her own field, in France influence as a sociologist depends to a much greater extent on one's prestige in matters of general culture that bridge specialized fields of study. The work must be accessible to the intellectuals, and "tout Paris" must know of and discuss it. When, therefore, Pierre Bourdieu publishes a large book on the social stratification of culture and taste, it is important not only as a piece of research but as a symbolic *objet* in its own right, to be read also for its meanings relevant to the politics of culture in France.

Distinction is extraordinary in its symbolic richness. It not only incorporates most of contemporary theory (including his friend Foucault's idea of power/knowledge); Bourdieu, like Goffman, has the capacity to say outrageous things in a manner sufficiently stylish and raised-eyebrow ironic that they can be heard sympathetically as academically proper savantry. Moreover, rare among theorists, Bourdieu is as sharp in his specific cultural insights as he is comprehensive in his theoretical reach. His outrageousness consists in his efforts to understand the tastes and other cultural choices of identifiable persons as dimensions of the distributive structure of cultural capital, the exercise of which, rooted as it is in the system of social stratification, contributes to its perpetuation. Which is real? The elite style or the critical/democratic substance? The answer is not important; the question is probably ill-posed. "Tout Paris" offered many answers, and that is exactly the point in writing an influential book. *Distinction* is a stunning virtuoso performance, enclosing within its wide embrace most of the important French intellectual constituencies while dampening some of its potential opposition. Its symbolism is a confirmation of its own thesis: it helped win for Bourdieu, against competition senior to him, his succession to Raymond Aron's chair at the Collège de France, the most prestigious in France. I cannot think of anyone who worked harder for it—or deserved it more.

7. I first read *Money, Morals, and Manners*, having previously read some of Michele Lamont's earlier work—for example, her article on Jacques Derrida, called "How to Become a Dominant French Philosopher," and her personal article describing her efforts to adapt to the culture shock of the transition from her Ph.D. work in Paris to a postdoc in the mathematics-dominated Stanford sociology department. It seemed likely to me, therefore, that she'd be a supremely "other directed" writer. And, in fact, at first glance her book seemed an almost paradigmatic lesson in How to Write an "Important" First Book and Get Tenure at a Major American University:

a. Bite off a BIG topic: a comparison of the culture of French and American upper-middle class men;

b. Do a lot of depth interviewing providing rich and quotable data that

c. Remind readers of a very successful and not entirely dissimilar recent book (*Habits of the Heart*);

d. In addition to the rich qualitative data from depth interviews, demonstrate your sampling and quantitative skills so as to anticipate critics who will predictably carp about the representativeness of the quotes from the depth interviews;

e. Use your findings to knock down a major theorist and senior researcher in your field (Bourdieu). Giant-killing is good practice for aspiring young academics. Besides, it will make you friends in Paris, where Bourdieu has enemies;

f. Don't offend those on whom your career does in fact depend. Therefore dampen the predominantly deterministic character of your analysis and play up the "relative autonomy of culture" theme;

g. Try for something conceptually innovative (like the "boundaries" idea—see below) and present it as something to replace the less comprehensive and less empirically adequate notions preceding it—like "cultural capital theory" (see point (e) above). Put these all together and you have the makings of a big book that will not fall between the cracks, will get respectfully noticed, and make a good reputation for a young scholar.

I don't in fact believe that Lamont's strategy was even nearly as calculated as the above suggests; it would be difficult to write so good a book with so calculated a strategy, and *Money, Morals, and Manners* is an impressive book, in spite of the few bones I have to pick with it. It aims to discover the differences and similarities in how men in the French and American upper middle class draw distinctions (or boundaries) of "worthiness" between themselves and others. They make these discriminations in terms of criteria Lamont calls "socioeconomic" (money/power), "cultural" (taste/aesthetic cultivation), or "moral" (e.g., honesty, integrity). Three major sorts of comparisons are made: between the French and the Americans in general; among the French and American residents of each nation's cosmopolitan urban areas (New York and Paris) and the residents of two comparable provincial cities (Indianapolis and Clermont-Ferrand); and between respondents in nonprofit and for-profit occupations within the upper middle class.

There are many findings reported, some major, some not, but I will cite only a few of them here. The French draw cultural boundaries more often than the Americans, but the residents in the provincial cities of both countries use cultural distinctions far less than the cosmopolitans. The French cosmopolitans invoke moral criteria less often than any of the other groups. Among the more interesting findings is the one that shows consistently more "liberal" attitudes among those who work in the nonprofit sector of the economy—a finding with a nice political edge that Lamont, regrettably, does little to hone any further.

Because the respondents are all upper middle class, class can't be used as an independent variable "determining" the vocabularies in which they say they make boundary distinctions. Nationality and cosmopolitan/provincial residence function here as independent variables affecting the frequency and distribution with which the three different criteria of judgment are invoked. But in many instances the differences turn out to be minor ones, and the closer one looks at the relative autonomy of the three criteria, the more blurred the boundaries they suggest become. "Worthiness," after all, is basically a moral concept, regardless of the vocabularies in which it is expressed.

In much of Bourdieu's work, for example, one gets the impression that the aesthetic ("cultural") discriminations made by his respondents are moral discriminations. "The style is the man," it is said, and for many people matters of taste *are* moral matters: bad taste in this view is a measure of *moral* inadequacy. As Lamont says, Americans are probably more tolerant of aesthetic diversity than the French, but tolerance of cultural diversity often disguises cultural indifference (characteristic of many Americans), and indifference permits a good bit of tolerance. There are, however, limits; where the aesthetic overlaps the moral (as it often does), for example in the continuing controversy over the NEA and "obscene" art, Americans can lose their tolerance rather quickly—which suggests blurred and fragile lines between the "moral" and the "cultural" criteria.

I see these criteria, or scales, as "manners of speaking," different modes of doing ideological work, in which cultural resources or repertoires are differently accessible to (and comfortable in the mouths of) those who invoke them. Lamont suggests, but does not fully exploit, the reasons that "moral" rhetorics are more comfortable for Americans than for the French: the Puritan tradition, perhaps; egalitarianism, certainly—but in a very specific sense. With few exceptions (like a ghettoed underclass) the great majority of Americans (despite significant class differences) have reasonably equitable access to a common "morality" (unlike Bernard Shaw's dustman in *Pygmalion* who could not "afford middle class morality," and was therefore cheerfully willing to sell his daughter to Professor Higgins for a price). Upper-middle-class Americans, (and perhaps the traditionalist Frenchmen of suburban Versailles) then, by sincerely invoking moral criteria they are materially equipped to live by, are in effect congratulating themselves while at the same time flashing their egalitarian credentials.

Indeed, I see all these manners of speaking (moral, socioeconomic, and cultural) as modes of self-congratulation—such values usually being group sustaining for collectivities and self-congratulatory for individuals. And the fact that, according to Lamont's own findings, "moral" criteria distinguish mainly an already familiar difference in sophistication between the French and the Americans in general (and the cosmopolitans and provincials in particular) suggests that the "moral" criteria may represent only a relatively easy and pious vocabulary invoked by those who aren't candid enough to use the tougher criteria of culture or socioeconomic achievement. "Honesty" and "integrity," after all, are porous and spongy enough terms to include (for some) Richard Nixon, Alan Cranston, Elliott Abrams, Jean-Marie le Pen and other honorable sleazes. The cultural and socioeconomic criteria are tougher because they almost necessarily imply certain levels of class or education; invoking those criteria has *costs* (you could be attacked as a snob, an elitist, or worse—admittedly more a problem in the U.S. than in France). Invoking moral criteria that command a broad consensus has virtually no cost, hence it's easy to do, and therefore of suspect validity.

The meaning of even the "socioeconomic" scale is ambiguous. Lamont notes that of those who use the socioeconomic criterion, some almost automatically infer a sort of moral criterion from it (richer, more powerful, or more accomplished people than I am are just better or superior people). There's a sense, then, in which all three scales constitute "moral" scales, but which indicate different kinds of moral vocabularies (or, as I say, manners of speaking). The analytic task for a sociologist is to connect causally these different manners of speaking to the different social locations of the subgroups of the sample. Lamont does this brilliantly in chapter 6 and parts of chapter 7 (where she analyzes the differences between the profit/nonprofit sectors). But then, in an apparent effort to appease the proponents of "multidimensional" theorizing and partisans of "agency," she rings the bell of "relative autonomy of culture," primarily by invoking the different "national traditions" of France and the U.S.

No doubt, the two countries have different national traditions, but the theoretical issue is not the national traditions differentiating the French bourgeoisie and the American upper middle class. Every middle class in each nation that has one probably has a tradition in some respects unique. American professors visiting France, for example, may be struck by the *ex*clusive character and atmosphere of French intellectual institutions: formidable walls and high iron fences; locked gates protecting its libraries and universities; remote and haughty staff demanding to see credentials before they'll break a smile. The culture conveys a symbolic "keep out unless you belong here." How different from the open, welcoming, *in*clusive culture of comparable American settings! French elitism versus American egalitarianism? To be sure. The relative safety from and vulnerability to terrorism in the two countries? Perhaps. But the point for a sociology of culture is to understand how these "national traditions" are created, invented, and sustained, and how they are placed under specific pressures to change by internal political conflicts and international markets, which affect all bourgeois institutions, though perhaps in different ways. In a number of places throughout her book Lamont notes marginally how French culture may be changing. But she doesn't use her sometimes sharp insights about that to conceive "national traditions" as historically deposited structures of culture that are subject to change as material pressures intensify. Nor, except for the category of profit/non profit employment, does she test for other more micro-structural variables to see how they might affect the ways in which her cosmopolitan and provincial respondents use the three scales of worthiness. Instead, she nearly reifies "national tradition" in behalf of an ambivalent effort to save some "autonomy" for cultural variables.

But, then, what exactly is it in the culture that Lamont's three scales of worthiness measure? It seems clear enough that by their different manners of speaking Lamont's respondents are doing ideological work, but it is not so clear if the symbolic boundaries they invoke represent actual social consequences like common club memberships, invitations to dinner, residential propinquity, intermarriage and so on: in short, a recurrently dense social life within the boundaries. We don't get much information about that.

Nor, except for some of the quotations themselves, do we get much insight into the *spirit* with which respondents say they use moral, cultural, or socioeconomic criteria in judging the worthiness of others— the more or less subtle overtones the spirit of the responses conveys to a careful listener. Are, for example, moral criteria invoked in a way that suggests that goodness is a transcendent quality of a spiritual elite? Or as simple virtue accessible even (perhaps especially) to the most humble? Or pragmatically—as in "honesty is the best policy"? The meaning of "moral" criteria depends on answers to these questions. Similarly, is the socioeconomic criterion invoked aggressively, suggesting hostility to or contempt for the high-minded claims of moral or cultural criteria? Or defensively, suggesting a felt sense of threat from other, perhaps competing, criteria? Or with cavalier confidence? Do those who invoke cultural criteria do so coarsely (are they climbers?) or modestly, even ironically, suggesting a certain reluctance (in the interests of "good taste") to appear to be brandishing them as credentials. In short, do the three scales invoke merely different criteria or are there real culture wars being waged by these different manners of speaking?

Lamont's data do not provide answers to such questions. When one interviews people about their judgments of others it seems prudent not to take what they say at face value, to maintain a certain skepticism about the answers one elicits. In making these judgments respondents also reveal the criteria by which they make them (some may not even have been previously aware of that), and expose themselves to criticism for the criteria they use. A certain posturing is thus to be expected, is perhaps almost inevitable because in responding one is not only offering a judgment but also implicitly defending the basis on which the judgment is made. Having clarified the basis of one's judgment, one does not usually want that clarity itself to render the judgment even more vulnerable to criticism than the previous obscurity. As Talcott Parsons once put it (presumably in defense of the dense turgidity of his own writing), "To be clear these days is to be found out."

I am not quite suggesting that one disbelieve one's own survey data, but I am suggesting adopting a skeptical posture toward them, knowing that I am thus violating one of the important assumptions of such research. For the question arises, why bother to do the research if one is not going to have confidence in its results? Because if one is not "sophisticated" about the kinds of questions that directly involve the self-image of respondents (and hence elicit responses that are, in effect, partly ideological posturings), the data one gets may not be valid, not responses to questions asked but to questions unasked. Most people do not lie very well, and when scholar-researchers who do their own interviewing are confronted with a posturing respondent, they are faced with the Hobson's choice of duly recording the lie or of not quite believing one's data. Hired-help interviewers are likely to opt for the former.

Why, then, does Lamont (who presumably did her own interviewing) choose not be skeptical about the ideological work done by her respondents? I think it's because their ideological work helps her to do her own. One of the most interesting things in her book is the way she uses the "boundaries" idea to mount a critique of Bourdieu's materialist theory of cultural capital. Lamont, for example, uses some findings from her book to criticize Bourdieu's neglect of "moral" categories of judgment, which he tends to see as epiphenomenal to more fundamental cultural and economic categories, that is, people use moral judgments as symbolic capital securing or enhancing their social status or economic position. Some of Lamont's respondents tell her that they make judgments of others in moral terms autonomous from cultural or socioeconomic ones, and that they tell her so Lamont regards as a major rent in the fabric of Bourdieu's understanding of how such distinctions are made.

She may well be right. But need we believe Lamont's respondents? Need she believe them? "We" (social scientists) are constrained to believe them because of a conventional stricture of research: once a survey is designed and under way, to rely exclusively on its findings to support or undermine whatever ideas are being explored or tested, and to avoid wherever possible bringing into the analytic process elements extraneous to the research itself (although footnotes may be used to cite other research supporting, extending, amending, or contradicting one's own findings, one of the several delights of Lamont's book). As a research genre the survey requires confidence in its findings.

Need Lamont herself believe her data? Well, she is constrained, like all of us, by the above considerations. But beyond this, it is clear in her book that Lamont *wants* to believe in the autonomy of moral criteria of judgment. Bourdieu's tendency to understand morality as a dimension or function of cultural or economic capital seems to her cynical, excessively worldly, too "Parisian" (which is why her research design includes provincial cities), a result of living too long in a hot-house atmosphere of ambitious intellectuals engaged in zero-sum struggles for status and power, rather than living among wholesome and ordinary middle class people for whom religion is salient and to whom morality is real and important.

Again, she may be right, but it's difficult to be confident about it given a measure of skepticism about the meaning of what respondents say. When interviewees tell researchers what they want to hear (and they almost always prefer to hear one thing rather than another), researchers do not often look that particular gift horse in the mouth—although it's good scientific practice to do exactly that. *Money, Morals, and Manners* is a very good book and a pleasure to read; it reveals a wealth of information about some of the cultural differences between the upper-middle-class males of France and the U.S. Lamont's confidence in these data (despite the grounds for skepticism I have described) enables her to assert the clarity and autonomy of three separate criteria of worthiness, the cosmopolitan bias in Bourdieu's thinking, and hence

the preferability of her more differentiated theory of symbolic boundaries to his theory of cultural capital. Pretty good ideological work,
I'd say.

8. Although all of the seven books discussed above represent mixed
genres (in the sense that they are not "purely" *Geisteswissenschaften* or
Naturswissenschaften) all of them lean in varying degrees toward the natural science end of the continuum; they are interested in how the pieces
of culture they study are determined or influenced (or resistant to influence) by the social structures in which the carriers of the culture are
embedded. *Habits of the Heart* (the phrase is from Tocqueville and the
authors see themselves as his intellectual heirs) is also a mixed genre but
of a different sort. The book's cultural focus is on American individualism, and although it was funded by several foundations, public and private, researched by highly qualified social scientists, and published by
an elite university press, it is not one of those books expected to sell
eight hundred or a thousand copies. In fact it became a best-seller, won
some prizes, and made a lot of money for its authors and publishers—
rather like some of its predecessors that sought both academic and non-
academic readers—for example, *White Collar, The Lonely Crowd,* and *The
Affluent Society.*

Why such popular success? In Clifford Geertz's terms the book is a
"blurred genre." It is a sociological study based on more than two hundred depth interviews with Americans from a variety of milieux (although no statistics are reported in the book). But it is also a tract; a
philosophical argument against the excesses of individualism in politics,
in the economy, and in the legendary heroes of American culture—
those Ahabs, Shanes, Deerslayers, and Sam Spades who find their ful-
fillment and identity in fleeing from social ties and from society itself
(heroes don't have to be home for dinner at an appointed hour or face
an angry spouse). As a tract, the book's ideological work is explicit and
deliberate. The authors argue that the "primary language" of Americans

is a language of utilitarian individualism whose excessive prevalence has weakened the "secondary language" of community (familial ties, civic duty, religious obligation) in which utilitarianism was rooted, and which made the individualism viable in the first place. In its conclusion the book calls for a restoration of community through a reappropriation of the traditions of republican virtue and religious obligation, by a renewal of the sense of vocation in work, greater commitment by corporations to the public good, and a decrease in the disparity between the rich and poor. It says little or nothing, though, about the structural conditions or legal constraints that might help to bring these about. Its strategy (unlike Luker's) is not empirical but hortatory. As a moral tract without political teeth, as cultural criticism that constitutes no threat to extant distributions of wealth or power, *Habits of the Heart* represents a genre that Americans have loved since the beginnings of the nation: the jeremiad. Like a Sunday sermon, it enables readers to feel morally uplifted for a while, then to return to continue their lives as before.

But *Habits of the Heart* is also a work of social science in which efforts are made to present evidence in behalf of its thesis with long quotations from the interviews, in which people talk about their marriages and careers, their community work, their ideals and frustrations, and their hopes for the future. A great strength of the book is that it is well written and clearly argued. But its greatest strength (and the greatest strength of much research of this kind) is its full and authentic evocation of individual persons struggling with the symbolic culture at their disposal to make sense of their lives and help solve their personal problems.

Although real persons are clearly evoked and real culture clearly rendered in *Habits of the Heart*, there is little sociology of the structuralist or determinist sort in it. We learn more than a little about the social backgrounds of the persons described; the authors, however, seem less interested in making any causal or functional assertions about the relation between the social location or milieu of their respondents and the symbolic culture at their disposal than in making a moral point about such relations. The clearest thing, for example, about their distinction between "communities" and "life-style enclaves" is their affirmation of the former and their disdain for the latter. There is a lot of culture described, evoked, interpreted, and even moralized in *Habits of the Heart*, but there is very little social structure in it; little systematic effort to connect the webs of social structure in which its interviewees are caught (even stuck) to the probabilities of them choosing this or that cultural strategy from the toolkit of culture that is made structurally available to them.

Early in the book, for example, there is an in-depth account of one of the interviewees, a hard-working business executive so driven by the need to succeed that he neglects his family—so much so that he is surprised and shaken when his wife leaves him and initiates divorce proceedings. We see him later, remarried, and devoting less attention to his career and more to his family—from which the authors invite readers to draw a moral lesson. What we readers do not learn is whether the man's career had perhaps plateaued, and whether the reduced prospects of further career advancement might have played some causal role in the diversion of his energies from work to family. What's missing in the analysis, in short, is some effort to connect moral choice (culture) to material interest.

If, as a tract, the ideological work of *Habits of the Heart* is explicit, as a work of social science its ideological work is somewhat hidden, and must be dug out. Early in the book the authors are a little apologetic about the predominantly middle-class character of the bulk of their respondents, but by the middle of the book they are making general assertions about "American" culture and individualism, apparently having forgotten the limitations of their sample. Of the some two hundred persons interviewed only twenty-five or so are at all vividly evoked; a large majority of those interviewed are not quoted in the book, and readers are told nothing about the principles of selection that guided the authors' choices about whom to quote. Of the interviews from which they do quote, the authors usually permit the quotations to be self-evidently moving and persuasive when they are told what they want to hear. But when they are told what they don't want to hear, the authors tend to do a lot of interpretive commentary to explain away what they are told—a common feature of research using depth interviews.

Moreover, the rhetorical style the authors adopt is what I call the seductive or royalist "we." The exemplar of this rhetoric is, of course, Lincoln's speech at the Gettysburg battlefield: the audience is directly addressed, as if speaker and listeners, author and readers constituted a community of belief engaged upon a joint moral enterprise (a device I myself have used in this very essay). Such rhetoric functions to induce (at least) or intimidate (at most) readers and listeners into believing that disagreement constitutes deviance from what that solidary "we" assumes is (or ought to be) a dominant consensus. Such language is basically moralist, seductive, religious; it generously invites audiences or readers into the believing community and hence dampens impulses to dissent; come, it says, let us believe together! It's no surprise, therefore, to discover that at least four of the five authors of *Habits* are persons of liberal religious belief who see the elite mainstream churches (among whom the book has had especially great success) as still the major institutional source of social (and therefore moral) commitment. Nor is it surprising that they neglect to note that the cultural traditions of Biblical individualism and republican virtue, although founded in rhetorics of egalitarianism and democracy, have in fact depended on hierarchy, authority, and inequality.

Let me make clear that I mostly agree with the book's thesis; aggressive individualism, perhaps best represented in the 1980s by its characterization as the age of greed, surely further weakened the sense of community to the point where those who merely hungered for it are now starved for it. Still, like its best-selling predecessors, at least the three that I mentioned above, the ideological work of *Habits of the Heart* was received far more favorably by the general public than by professional social scientists—which suggests that there are still formidable barriers to satisfying both constituencies simultaneously.

9. In 1986 Ann Swidler, one of the junior authors of *Habits of the Heart*, published in the American Sociological Review what is arguably the definitive theoretical essay ("Culture in Action") characterizing culture as an active component of behavior rather than as a "dependent variable." Joining Geertz, she moves the discussion of culture away from the Parsonian emphasis on values. She conceives culture as a symbolic toolkit providing people with the techniques, the rhetorical means, and other resources for choosing effective "strategies of action" to help them cope with the worlds they inhabit. Given this emphasis on the active agency of culture, it is not surprising that Swidler pays little attention to how those tools, means, and other resources are made available and accessible to those who use them, nor to how choices (which usually imply "values") from the range of accessible strategies are shaped by social placement.

That perspective, I think, is intimately connected with the *kind* of research Swidler typically (and usually superbly) does: depth interviews, like those in *Habits of the Heart*, in which people open up and provide rich, complex, and highly personal information about themselves. In a larger, book-length empirical study of the culture of love and marriage based on such interviewing, Swidler introduces a distinction between romantic love and what she calls "prosaic love," the latter characteristic of long-married couples who have to "work at" keeping their marriages and households together. She seems more interested in examining prosaic love than romantic love. Although she does point out that romantic love functions to motivate people to marry, she does not seem to see the structurally all-but-mandatory character of romantic love in this process. Romantic love is how modern societies "arrange" marriage: by inducing young people to fall in love with proper others. We are continually reminded by both popular and elite media that those who have never been in love have missed the best that life has to offer—which is a strong incentive to fall in love and an intimidation to those who have not, who may thus be shamed by a presumed "incapacity to love."

For Swidler, romantic love is "mythic," but prosaic love is a practical instrument in the cultural toolkit, a strategy that enables marriages to endure by providing spouses with a usable vocabulary to negotiate the terms of their continuing partnership. Mature married couples work at their marriages in order to sustain marriage as an institution. Romantic love and prosaic love are equally chunks of culture for Swidler, but only romantic love is mythic. She apparently does not see that prosaic love may be fully as mythic—only a different myth whose significance lies in its relevance to sustaining marriages already made rather than in making new ones. For mature married couples who find it necessary to "work at" their marriages, they must legitimate that work by inventing ideologies that sanctify it, and myths are powerful sanctifiers.

Seeing the matter this way has the merit of sensitizing a student of love to variations in the two myths. Empirically speaking, Swidler cites no evidence to suggest that *in fact* people who work at their marriages have more enduring partnerships than those who don't. It may be that spouses whose romantic passion for each other survives long years of marriage will be less likely to emphasize "working at" it than spouses whose passion for each other has cooled. That, at least, has the merit of being a testable hypothesis—even if it turns out to be wrong. In one particularly pointed interview, Swidler encounters a woman whose passion for her husband has not cooled after several years of marriage. But the woman is inarticulate about it; she can't talk; her responses are the equivalent of "I don't know, I just love him." Swidler regards this as a bad interview; she couldn't get much from the respondent, and she sees this particular marriage as culturally impoverished because the wife cannot speak articulately about her feelings. What I see here is not impoverishment but a woman in possession of a culture that says one is not *supposed* to talk rationally about one's sexual passion; there's no publicly acceptable language for such talk—particularly to an interviewer-stranger. There *is* an institutionally accepted language for talking about prosaic love and working at marriages.

Swidler doesn't see it this way, I think, because she has an unadmitted and perhaps unrecognized bias in favor of prosaic love. She is, after all, a professor at an elite university married to another elite professor; she is the mother of a child and belongs to the generation for whom working at marriages combined with careers and motherhood is very much part of an upper-middle-class culture they share. Her analysis of prosaic love is unconvincing not because it doesn't exist there in the toolkit of culture; of course it exists. It's unconvincing because she seems to have been looking for exactly that tool to deal with her own preconceptions of what mature married commitment is about. It's no surprise that she found it. But note again: like any research finding that confirms an investigator's preconceptions, it tends to be treated in an uncritical manner. She misses, in short, the ideological work contained in the concept of prosaic love because she agrees with it; it is *her* ideology. Hence she misses the fact that the prose of married love is fully as mythic as the poetry of romantic love. They function in different ways for different stages of the life-marriage cycle.

Because she's fond of prosaic love, she also misses the theme of defensive disappointment it contains—rather like those parents who, when interviewed about their occupational hopes for their children, reply, "I want them to be whatever they want to be," thus brushing on a patina of permissive or voluntarist rhetoric to disguise their actual powerlessness to determine their children's occupational futures.

Like *Habits of the Heart*, the greatest strength of Swidler's research is the rich data generated by the long and detailed interviews. Individuals are evoked with great complexity, and we can see empirically what Swidler, Bellah et al., and other students of culture who use depth interviews insist upon generally: that people are not inert, passive objects buffeted about by the variety of forces and constraints to which they are structurally subjected. We see people who are active, intentional, subtle, culturally skilled—so much so that it's almost an impertinence even to think of looking for structurally predictable patterning in the utilization of the cultural strategies at their disposal. The price, in short, of these culturally rich descriptions is the poverty of any causal or functional analysis relating symbolic structure to social structure. I think, in fact, that the strategy of depth-interview researchers, in resisting what they take to be the passive or inert image of human beings in the work of those seeking causal determinate relations, is exactly to evoke the depth and complexity of personal culture, and, therefore, to make structuralist efforts at causal generalization seem shallow, simple, and banal by comparison. I think, too, that they are right; most research aiming at causal generalization about the relations between symbolic structure and social structure *is* superficial and banal by comparison with the rich portraits of inner lives that emerge from depth interviews and from extended ethnographic observation. But that is not really the point. That the disparate modes of research use their distinctive strengths to do different kinds of ideological work (and hence sometimes generate antagonisms) should not obscure their complementary roles in serious efforts to seek general truths about culture and social life.

14 / MIXED GENRES, METAPHYSICAL PATHOS, IDEOLOGICAL WORK

Readers will have noticed that I have been conducting two apparently contradictory (or at least usually opposed) lines of argument. One line insists on a scientific approach to the study of culture; a sociology of culture is properly preoccupied not only with descriptive/interpretive accounts of symbolic meanings but with causal explanations connecting symbolisms to the social structures in which carriers of symbolisms (i.e., people) are embedded. But in examining the nine good pieces of research analyzed in section 13 (and I have deliberately selected good work rather than bad) I have also argued that they all do ideological work, which, the conventional wisdoms that contrast science and ideology still insist, weakens their claims to constitute reliable knowledge.

I think the two lines of argument are complementary. When I was regularly teaching contemporary theory to new graduate students one of the things I insisted that students attend to in their reading was what Alvin Gouldner (adapting Arthur Lovejoy's idea) called the "metaphysical pathos" of the theorist: that central infrastructure of concern that informed the theorist's major work and drove him to write. This is the sensibility that a reader finds more or less attractive or unattractive in the text: Weber's gloom about rationalization; Durkheim's prescient concern with morality as social health; Parsons's obsession with seeing order wherever he looked—even with deviance and other bizarrerie; the Frankfurt School's furtively elitist understanding of mass culture and technology as dehumanization; Goffman's refusal to protect even the most minute part of the "self" from sociology; and so on. Sometimes you have to read between lines to get a sense of that, or know something about who the writer's sometimes invisible antagonists are. Getting the metaphysical pathos right was important because it was a genuine reading aid, getting you through the dry stretches, the obscurity, the pedantry in even the best of theorists.

Getting the metaphysical pathos right was for me an essential element of learning to read critically. But whereas that practice is conventional in literary studies, and sometimes acceptable in assessing theory, it is not regarded as entirely legitimate in the criticism of empirical social science research, where conventional proprieties limit (note the reification in that phrase) legitimate criticism of the assertions in the work to how well its data and research methods support its assertions—as if the sensibilities of social science writers were irrelevant to the critical tasks at hand. Weber reminded readers of "value *relevance*" (that research was relevant to values) but nevertheless insisted on what became an orthodoxy of objectivity: that the validity of factual findings could be assessed independently of the values that may have inspired the research.

This was formulated nearly a hundred years ago, however, and since then (and accelerating since the sixties) influential arguments have been made weakening the foundation of that orthodoxy, which, as an orthodoxy, constituted very successful ideological work. In the 1930s, Parsons emphasized in his famous definition of "fact" the contingency of its placement "in terms of a conceptual scheme"; ethnomethodologists emphasized the social construction of facts, the creation of documents (and their selective survival) for social purposes including both the falsification and the accurate recording of events; critics of survey research have shown how consensus and "common sense" (i.e., pieces of culture) shape the codes in terms of which survey data are classified and given meaning; Thomas Kuhn in his landmark work on scientific revolutions revealed the role of "paradigms" in shaping routine science, and the role of scientific communities in sustaining paradigms; current work in science studies (particularly by the "strong programme" of David Bloor and the Edinburgh group of sociologists) focuses on the typical interpenetration of social networks, politics, alliances, fund-raising, and other social forces with scientific work narrowly conceived. And finally, Clifford Geertz (who else?) published *Works and Lives* in 1988 focusing, of all things, on the *sensibilities* of several major modern anthropologists as writers.

While such work has not been entirely successful in creating a new orthodoxy, it has somewhat weakened the absoluteness of the old orthodoxy separating facts from values; it at least suggests some of the contingencies of that orthodoxy and its dependence on a variety of prior assumptions embedded in both the general culture and the specific subcultures of science and scholarship. Moreover, much of this kind of thinking may be called poststructuralist (if not postmodernist) in its efforts to "deconstruct" what had been socially constructed (and then taken for granted). Still, it is well to remember that, though the name is recent, deconstruction has been a recurrent practice of intellectuals for a very long time, especially when engaging in criticism of extant conventional wisdoms. Marx did it; Nietzsche did it. It is a typical move for intellectuals embarked on theoretical innovation to deconstruct (by shifts of perspective or challenges to implicit premises) the plausibility of the wisdoms expressed by the targets of their criticism. Big deconstructions produce big critical reputations—for example, Foucault's. After laying out deconstruction in purely abstract terms, he applied them to family, sex, prisons, and hospitals, very big issues indeed. Smaller deconstructions produce smaller reputations—for example, ethnomethodology's critical analysis of the routine use by sociologists of such basic concepts as status and role.

Although blowing the cover on conventional wisdoms is usually associated with an avant-garde or cultural Left, deconstruction is not the exclusive property of the Left. The attack from the Right on "political correctness," for example, deconstructs some of the tired and reified clichés of the Left. Invoked by the Left or Right, however, deconstruction almost always has a critical edge; someone's conceptual ox is being gored. In the conduct of this particular cultural war the aim is usually to weaken or paralyze your opponent's thinking by attacking it at its source. All combatants are vulnerable in this war because we all need relatively undeconstructed concepts to think with. When those foundations are nibbled away or cut off clean with the stroke of a metaphoric machete, one may be left feeling very threatened indeed—which may help explain why so many hard scientists so highly placed in the academic order of precedence have reacted with such panicked hostility to the relativizing implications of historians and sociologists of science, men and women with relatively little prestige in academic hierarchies (Gross and Levitt 1994).

That science (soft science more obviously, but hard science too) does ideological work, then, is not necessarily a weakness or a contradiction. The metaphysical pathos informing a piece of work often constitutes a source of its distinctive strength and importance, though it may also render it vulnerable to criticism. "Realist" philosophies of science are usually informed by a metaphysical desire to justify established scientific practice as the best and purest way of discovering general truths about nature or society, though there may be some "bad faith" indicated by a reluctance to admit that the desire is at work in the argument as well as logic and evidence. Relativist and quasi-relativist views of science are usually informed by a desire to reveal scientific practice (and art) as another form of human work, more disciplined than most, perhaps, but shot through with the same sort of human frailties and historical contingencies that characterize other occupations and professions—though there may be some bad faith indicated by a reluctance to admit to the delight often taken in deflating the reigning orthodoxies.

Note, however, that though their metaphysical pathos is sharply different, the two sensibilities may find themselves agreeing on the warrant for the empirical claims in a piece of research, *in spite of disagreeing about the bases of the warrant.* Realists may warrant an empirical claim as an accurate representation of nature or social life in its objective reality; others may, more modestly, rest content with historical and sociological accounts of how empirical claims come to be warranted—including the ideological credentials displayed by the work to its warranting communities. I know of no scientific method for proving the preferability of one view to the other.

A distinction between good and bad (or better and worse) ideological work is relevant here. Philosophies of science are ideologies (arguments promoting or defending ideal and material interests), and some of them are very good indeed. Warranting communities, as "social constructions," are not built of equally sturdy materials. As that huffing and puffing wolf discovered, some edifices are built of straw and others of brick. Some social constructions have lasted as long as human history; others collapse if you look at them funny. A long-lasting paradigm in science probably indicates very good ideological work done in its behalf (and the sturdiness of the social structures—warranting communities—that sustain its orthodoxies), although as Kuhn suggests, the accumulation of anomalies (which may require struggle among professionals even to be recognized as "anomalies") will eventually generate the development of new paradigms and new ideological work. Models of social science research are far less sturdy, their warranting communities more diverse, and their ideological work therefore more visible.

This, I think, is one of the meanings of Bourdieu's helplessly ironic remark that there is no way out of the culture game. To write about culture (including the culture of science) is to write about matters central not only to one's interests but also to one's very sense of self. The ideological work may express one's own deep values (as in Swidler's work and in *Habits of the Heart*) or career exigencies attached to "schools of thought" (as in Lamont's book or Jackson's), or it may lie in the objectivist strategies that function as self-protective devices against potentially volatile controversy (as in Luker's and Mukerji's work), or the ambivalent resistance to the claims of both the dominant culture and "deviant" cultures or subcultures (as in my own research as well as Willis's and, to some extent, Bourdieu's). To write about culture is inevitably to leave work for one's critics to do; there is no "last word" in matters like these.

These considerations may well represent limitations on some of the claims of a piece of work to constitute conclusive knowledge, but they do not rob the work of its cogent or lasting contributions. To say that scholarly academic work does ideological work is not to say that's all it does. Individualist achievement won at the cost of community or family solidarity often does weaken groups and leaves the achiever feeling betrayed (sometimes with no unambiguously visible blame to place); "working at" routinized marriages *has* become an institutionalized cultural resource for coping with high divorce rates at a time when divorce has lost most of its stigma; dominant classes *do* stigmatize the cultural tastes of subordinate classes; there *are* systematic cultural differences between the French and American upper middle class and systematic differences of social placement between pro-choice and pro-life women; and all of us must cope with the recurrent problems of everyday life (like child rearing) under conditions in which the culture (in an age of science) "demands" informed decisions but in which conclusive knowledge on which to base those decisions is at best fragile and incomplete or simply not there.

The research works that I have scrutinized here, then, constitute mixed or blurred genres; they are neither purely "positivist" nor "humanist," neither purely *Geisteswissenschaft* nor *Naturswissenschaft*, although each may be placed closer to one or the other ideal-typical pole. Nor do they constitute art, science, philosophy, or journalism, although pieces of them may be beautiful, true, profound, or topical. They are mixed genres, what we call "social science," cultivated primarily by academics, usually for other academics in circumstances where no single paradigm rules unchallenged and no single set of critical criteria commands unanimous assent. The same work may be praised for its rigor or criticized for its banality, praised for its timeliness or criticized for its ephemerality, praised for its scope and reach or criticized for its vagueness or its uncertain grasp, praised for its technical precision or criticized for its jargon, praised for its relevance to important issues or criticized for its bias. Unlike the "hard" sciences (where questions that are in principle empirical are routinely rejected as "unscientific" or premature when there are no available means of answering them conclusively), social sciences routinely conduct and publish research on questions the answers to which will predictably evoke criticism and controversy (very few books in the social sciences get unanimously rave reviews) in proportion to the impact of the answers on established interests.

This is especially the case in studies of culture (the walking-on-eggs problem), not only, as I suggested earlier, because the intellectuals who do this work tend to be a bit vain about the autonomy of their efforts, but also because we are so plainly involved in and part of the culture we study, have interests in what we conclude from those studies, and cannot reasonably expect those interests to be ignored by critics with perhaps opposing interests. Nor can we expect (though we can hope for) the kind of relentless reflexivity that continually turns back on its own convictions and interests to reflect on where they came from and on how they affect the work at hand. Few people have interests in such reflexivity; the result is often uncertainty, anomie, even intellectual paralysis.

3

Structure and Choice in Sociology

15 / CULTURE AND ENCHANTMENT

The mixing of genres described above constitutes the bad news for Mark Schneider. In a brilliantly written and argued recent book, *Culture and Enchantment*, Schneider is made distinctly uncomfortable by mixed genres. He sets up an invidious distinction between what he calls "naturalist discourse" and "edifying discourse." Naturalist discourse is the language of science, edifying discourse the language of culture, and ne'er the twain shall meet. The basic reason for this separation of realms of discourse is that the data of culture are "enchanted." They are inherently mercurial and ambiguous, subject to a variety of interpretations; they will not sit still to be studied. This isn't, of course, true of all culture. Some pieces of culture, as Schneider admits, are simple and relatively stable; the meaning of giving someone "the finger" is clear and unambiguous as a symbolic gesture—or in Schneider's example, the thumb-against-the-teeth. Schneider, however, is interested in rich, subtle, and complex culture, full of opacity and obscurity, and he finds such phenomena unamenable to naturalist (causal-explanatory) analysis—one of his cases in point being the poetry of Mallarmé, although much of modernist or postmodernist literature would do as well.

No doubt there are extremes of opacity and obscurity in such literature (as there are in nature) but there are many classic works of literature (and collective literary traditions) that command high degrees of consensus among literature's warranting communities on what they mean—and perhaps even higher degrees of consensus on what they *don't* mean. I'm reminded here of Lionel Trilling's young English literature instructor (in his story "Of This Time, of That Place") lecturing an aggressive undergraduate on the limits of relativism regarding an interpretation of Wordsworth (several interpretations may be possible, he tells the student, but not yours). Nor is a sociology of literature-as-culture centrally concerned with the analysis of specific individual works; that's what literary critics usually do, and they usually do it better than sociologists. Bourdieu's recent book on Gustave Flaubert, for example, is less concerned with "explaining" *Madame Bovary* than with the conditions that enabled Flaubert to play an important part in altering the milieu and the aesthetics of the French novel, the "field" in which French novelists practice their craft.

Similarly, it's not only symbolically "poor" stuff (like giving someone "the finger") whose meaning is unambiguous. There are many chunks of culture considerably richer and more complex that are not thereby impossibly ambiguous or mercurial. Erving Goffman was perhaps the greatest single virtuoso at detecting the social order and ritual meaning in subtle pieces of complex culture, and he was particularly good at naming these phenomena, like "tie signs" and "civil inattention." Sexual signaling, for example, is a rich and subtle piece of local culture, and, if they've been trained from an early age to decipher the code, most people most of the time (sociology is a probabilistic discipline) get it right despite its complexity. These are matters of degree. There are unplumbed, and possibly unplumbable, mysteries in culture—as there are in nature; perhaps more in nature than in culture. But that cultural objects keep accumulating—and losing—symbolic meaning does not preclude those changes being studied naturalistically. Even when there aren't high degrees of consensus about meaning, the variations are seldom random. If "attitudes" are pieces of internalized culture, then the bulk of survey research on attitudes may be understood as an effort to explain their variation, plurality, and mercuriality. Indeed, if it seems odd that attitude researchers are not usually regarded (nor regard themselves) as sociologists of culture it is very likely because their methods are usually positivist whereas most sociologists of culture typically adopt anti-positivist research postures. It seems clear, nevertheless, that survey research on attitudes is designed to disclose the social structuring of culture.

Schneider, then, may have thrown in the towel on a sociology of culture prematurely. His dichotomies between edification and naturalism, explanation and interpretation, hermeneutics and science, meaning-as-intention and meaning-as-interpretation seem to invite his conclusion that the two modes of knowing go their epistemically segregated ways. There is a rather strict formalism working here, disdainful of the mixed genres I have described. If, as Schneider admits, meaning-as-intention can be studied naturalistically, why not meaning-as-interpretation? The answers that Schneider gives (mercuriality of the data, lack of consensus) are, as I have suggested, arguable. Cultural objects accumulate (and lose) meaning over time through changing contextual influences on the interpretations that get attached to and loosened from them by the actions of potentially identifiable persons and groups. This process is revealed in both Paul Dimaggio's and Larry Levine's work on high and low culture and in large measure is what Bourdieu's work is about. Bourdieu is particularly insistent on the point that the persisting enchantment—even mystification—of culture is less a matter of the nature of the data than of the fact that lots of identifiable people have material and ideal interests (macro-political ones and micro-personal ones) in resisting or opposing naturalist (sociological) understandings of culture. If cultural phenomena are *defined* by their symbolic character, then it takes a lot of interpretive work even to get a handle on the "objects" you might want to explain in naturalist terms. Here is Goffman on sexual signaling:

> The initiator exposes himself to rejection and to the judgment that he is undesirable, which judgment anyone who keeps his distance is allowed to avoid; the recipient exposes herself to providing personal evidence of another's desirability without obtaining the relationship that is the usual safeguard of this admission. The solution is strategic tact. The initiator undertakes to be tentative enough and discourageable enough so that if he is to be rejected, this can be done delicately, by indirection as it were, allowing him to maintain the line

that no overture had been intended. And the recipient when desiring to encourage an overture does so in a manner that can be seen as mere friendliness should the need arise to fall back on that interpretation. . . . An ambiguity thus results, but this derives not from some lack of consensus, failure of communication, or breakdown in social organization, but from competent participation in the relationship game.

In this little scene (which, even in 1994, is not likely to be regarded as sexual harassment) Goffman displays his virtuoso gifts for extracting the cultural order and meaning in a complex and subtle slice of recurrent ritual interaction. Schneider, however, seems to distrust virtuosity. His use of the word retains some of the pejorative connotations of seventeenth-century usage when it implied a certain lack of gravity, a soupçon of dilettantism, eccentricity, or showiness, the antithesis of the stolid solidity he associates with "mature" naturalist science. Contemporary usage, however, usually conveys unambiguous praise (as in virtuoso performances by musicians—Isaac Stern, Artur Rubenstein, Art Tatum, Wynton Marsalis—or actors, say Dustin Hoffman in *Midnight Cowboy, Tootsie,* or *Rainman*). Schneider's discomfort with virtuosity is particularly evident in his discussions of Geertz (surely an interpretive virtuoso in this performance sense) and Lévi-Strauss (also a virtuoso) both of whose discourse Schneider finds ambiguous, most of it edifying while apparently making naturalist claims. There is no doubt that he appreciates their intellectual gifts but he is put off by the ambiguity of their "epistemic register" (a nice sonic metaphor), which offends his sense of the proper separation between enchanted and disenchanted realms, between edifying and naturalist discourse.

Schneider's apparent identification of virtuosity with edifying discourse in the cases of Geertz and Lévi-Strauss is, I think, a mistake. Paul Lazarsfeld, for example, was also a virtuoso, but clearly a naturalist virtuoso because of his endlessly inventive searches for ways of quantitatively testing difficult-to-specify relationships among variables. Lazarsfeld was able to teach students his analytic techniques but, like Geertz and Lévi-Strauss (and Goffman) he couldn't pass on his originality or virtuosity to his students. Whether the virtuosity of Geertz or Lévi-Strauss is or is not properly a term of praise remains itself an epistemically ambiguous matter for Schneider. Is this ambiguity a cognitive vice? I'm not sure that Schneider has his mind completely made up about this. He treats Geertz's ambiguity as evasiveness or contradiction, and Lévi-Strauss's as theoretical flights of fancy with little hope of empirical test. Yet he acknowledges that they are the two most influential anthropologists of our time—and in a discipline whose dominant epistemic register (although under a lot of challenge now from the "new anthropology") is still naturalist! It won't do to call cultural anthropology irrevocably enchanted when most of its senior scholars still prize heavy documentation for every assertion, and cross-cultural testing of every effort at generalization. How did these two edifying anthropologists become so influential in spite of their discipline's dominant epistemology?

We can conceivably try to understand this sort of thing by perhaps beginning with edifying (interpretive) discourse, and gradually moving toward a naturalist hypothesis. For example: elite sociologists and anthropologists have relatively short career trajectories; the best of them are usually as famous and prestigious as they're ever going to be by the time they reach their late forties or early fifties. If by then they have achieved all or most of the rewards their discipline is capable of conferring (or that they want from it), the discipline loses a lot of its social control over them, and they become relatively free to seek further recognition and prestige (or money and power for that matter) from new reference groups or warranting communities, say, in university administration, government, or politics; or in the arts and humanities, in philosophy and belles lettres (as Geertz has apparently done)—which disciplines are older and in some respects more prestigious than sociology or anthropology. As professional groups, sociologists and anthropologists are, save for the relatively few exceptions at the top, neither very cultivated nor broadly and humanistically educated. So it's not hard for their senior elites to get bored with their whole mainstream enterprise *once they've achieved renown within it;* perhaps a more advanced version of the Groucho Marx/Woody Allen syndrome: where they wouldn't be a member of any club that would accept them, our two elite anthropologists may wear their membership lightly when grander memberships beckon. Under such conditions, blurred genres or epistemic ambiguity can seem rather attractive, particularly when extant orthodoxies are under challenge and alternate warranting communities are available and receptive.

In his 1988 book, *Works and Lives,* for example, Geertz seems to opt for that ambiguous cognitive space between ethnography and literary analysis. In considering the writing of several influential anthropologists, his focus is on the style and sensibility evident in their texts. For him, the "problem" of ethnography is not epistemological but literary: how convincingly ethnographers transform their experience of fieldwork among exotics ("being there") into prose written primarily for their unexotic colleagues ("being here"). Like Erving Goffman who, late in his career, seems to have felt threatened by the prospect of ethnomethodology usurping what had been preeminently Goffman's "turf" (i.e., micro-sociology), Geertz adopts the posture of an elder gently but severely lecturing his younger colleagues ("the new anthropology") on having gone too far in the direction (ethnographers front and center, invisible no more; reflexive and angst-ridden about whether they know what they claim to know) that he himself pioneered. Geertz's analysis of ethnographic writing is aestheticized and contains an aversion to political statement. The "political" becomes for him almost an equivalent of the coarse or the vulgar; whether it's the egalitarian or left sympathies of some of the "new" ethnographers or the naive liberalism of Ruth Benedict's "upward and onward" theme, Geertz's disdain is palpable. Although he distances himself too from Evans-Pritchard's Bwana mentality, he admires the confidence it lends to his prose (better than the wimpy self-doubts of reflexivity), in which "an honest story honestly told" is evident. That "honest story" is as close as Geertz comes to an epistemological criterion for assessing ethnographies, as if an honest story honestly told could not possibly be just plain wrong, instead of "another part of the elephant."

Can I boil this edifying talk down to a testable proposition? Try this: more elite social scientists than journeymen will in late career write increasingly in epistemically ambiguous registers. That's a step toward "explaining" Geertz's work since the research in Morocco and Indonesia that made his early reputation. And for Lévi-Strauss (as a French intellectual) that broadening is probably de rigueur. In France you don't get to the top of your field without your work being known and appreciated by intellectuals outside of it. In that sense, Geertz is "very French." The proposition may turn out to be false, but its merit lies both in its falsifiability and its emergence from my own edifying discourse. Good hypotheses do not drop from the sky. So rather than see interpretation and explanation condemned to invidiously segregated realms of intellectual work, it seems more prudent to understand both as essential steps toward sociological understandings of culture—which, at their best, will be both naturalist and edifying.

The edifying parts will of course contain some ideological work. In my counterculture book I regarded that as a problem, and used a reflexive strategy in an effort to neutralize it while reminding my readers that the reflexivity itself was, inevitably, a form of ideological work. I also adopted an autobiographical style of reporting and interpreting ethnographic data in order to convey to readers information about the circumstances of my life that may have tilted my analysis in ways I was not aware of (and hence could not be reflexive about). Although I still use these practices, it seems to me that they reveal efforts to detach oneself from ideology for the sake of an utterly pure image of science that, unfortunately, matches no real social science I know of. It is as if by reflexivity's attempt at continual purification and repurification of thought, an icy selfless detachment could be attained, rather like Weber's ideal of objectivity, the eradication of self sought by some Eastern religions, or those orthodox American Freudians who, in the name of pure therapy, congratulate themselves on their cold resistance to efforts by patients to engage them in any humanly sympathetic interaction.

Over the last several years I have been wondering if this search for purity—in scientific detachment, therapeutic asceticism, academic neutrality, aesthetic distance—does not represent still another illusion about the ethereality of culture, involving either an effort to transcend engagement with the social world or to manifest an heroic detachment from or indifference to it. In this context I have been impressed with the work of Howard Becker on art worlds and Bruno Latour on science worlds, who treat the practices of artists and scientists as they would any other occupation that requires cooperation, collaboration, and allies in order to reach its audiences and to be found credible or otherwise worthy. For these scholars successful work in art or science *always* involves an impure combination of cognitive, aesthetic, political, economic, and ideological skills not only difficult to disentangle but whose very disentanglement could be counterproductive for understanding the enterprises of art and science fully. For Becker, an aesthetic force is not more powerful than the organizational and distributive forces that bring an aesthetic to its audiences. For Latour the force of a scientist's experiment is not greater than the funding savvy and the political skills that made the experiment possible nor the networks of allies and warranting communities through which discoveries are sympathetically diffused and achieve status as definitive knowledge.

Although not without some problems of their own, these works have the merit of an utterly pragmatic, matter-of-fact approach to quasi-sacred topics. By revealing the everyday worlds of artists and scientists, Becker and Latour contribute to the demystification of their image of purity, and therefore weaken the hegemony of the chunks of culture they represent. They do that ideological work very well. Such sociologies of culture are, I think, informed by an anti-hegemonic spirit or metaphysical pathos. Unlike *Habits of the Heart* (which affirms a dominant middle-class culture of civility), these are works of cultural deviance—

though not of political radicalism. By connecting social structures to symbolic structures they promote the transformation of culture into ideologies, consent into contest, unity into diversity, and traditional consensus into points of view that need to be defended with reason and evidence.

16 / CAUSALITY AND CULTURE

In an article on rational choice thinking a few years back in the *New Republic* (Hawthorn, 1990), there was a reference to James Duesenberry, the economist who had said that economics was about how people make choices and sociology was about how they don't have any choices to make—one of those benign exaggerations in behalf of a point worth exaggerating. Tocqueville said man is partly determined, partly free. Durkheim spoke of the simultaneous interiority and exteriority of culture; that institutions form us and that we form institutions. Marx told us that we make our own history, though not under conditions we have freely chosen. I think that these familiar notions have become comforting clichés that discourage us from pushing for answers to the empirical questions they invite. How much free? How much determined? How do the conditions we do not control shape the kinds of history we are free to make? What conditions obstruct or facilitate our capacity to shape institutions? How is it that some of us are more resistant, more recalcitrant than others to being shaped by institutions?

Determinism and freedom should be boring issues for sociologists because they are fundamentally metaphysical. People care about whether they *feel* free or trapped, or somewhere in-between. Under what conditions do we feel free? Under what like pawns? It seems plain enough that both occur, sometimes simultaneously, and our language reflects that fact. Are we determined? Our common languages are full of conventional expressions testifying to that condition: I did what I was told; I had no other choice; the pressure was too great to do otherwise; I was between a rock and a hard place; my position requires that I . . .

and so on. Note that these expressions are common in a context of apology for the limiting constraints on one's action. But this language of constraint and necessity is not always used apologetically. Remember the cliché: a man's gotta do what a man's gotta do. Here, the language of necessity expresses a consummation, a moral triumph; expressive freedom *as* necessity—although when we feel free we are usually reluctant to hear what may have determined that feeling. It's also true that our languages are full of the vocabularies of choice, agency, voluntarism, individualism. Neither the vocabularies of constraint nor those of choice, it seems to me, should be taken at face value; there are both clear and obscure reasons for people to speak disingenuously about the relative constraints on or freedom of their choices. In a culture like ours (that celebrates freedom) most people much of the time are likely to grouse about or be reluctant to face the fact of the constraints on their freedoms; it takes a kind of mysterious cognitive blip or cultural redefinition of the situation to put groups in a mood where protest or complaint against restrictions on their freedom seem legitimate rather than like mere whining. Even when they are not disingenuous, persons are seldom fully aware of the deepest social sources from which their most authentic tastes, feelings, and choices spring, and they often don't even desire that awareness—called "self-consciousness," a phrase that carries with it its connotation of awkward embarrassment.

The problem for research on such matters is still to connect specific courses of action to specific structures of incentive and constraint in such a way that the magnitudes of felt freedom and unfreedom are (probabilistically) "determined" outcomes of the interaction between the "pull" of personal and group interests generated by social location and the "push" of accessible culture or ideologies (cognitive, moral, aesthetic) in terms of which any course of action must be justified to its probable proponents, and defended against its probable critics and opponents. Where the pushes and pulls are homogeneous or consistently unidirectional the magnitudes of felt constraint are likely to be minimal; rhetoric is likely to be eloquent and righteous, and action is likely to be sure, firm, and feel free (like Luker's abortion activists, Willis's working-class boys, and Ann Swidler's couples who "work at" their marriages). In such instances culture and material interests are likely to be so reciprocally interpenetrated as to seem given, natural.

But where the pushes and pulls are heterogeneous, multidirectional, or contradictory (perhaps in what Swidler calls "unsettled lives"), rhetoric is likely to be halting, banal, sheepish, clumsy, defensive, or ambiguous; action is likely to be ambivalent, anguished, perhaps paralyzed. The sense of autonomy is dimmed; one feels acted upon rather than acting, determined rather than free (like Willis vis-à-vis his "lads" or Luker vis-à-vis her abortion activists or me vis-à-vis communards or some of "the new ethnographers"). Material and ideal interests are working at cross purposes, and pressure will be felt to alter one or the other or both.

I think we know more than a little about some of the conditions under which people feel relatively free and unconstrained, and about the conditions under which they're likely to feel like *things*, buffeted about by history, circumstance, and other puppet-masters. To say that the pushes and pulls are mostly homogeneous means that an individual or collective actor's interests are not in major conflict with each other, and that legitimation is taken for granted, a matter of shared, self-evident culture. To say that the pushes and pulls are multidirectional or contradictory means that an actor's interests *are* in some major conflict with each other, and that legitimacy is no longer a matter of shared culture but of legitimately contested ideologies. I think too that a determinist sociology has some small role to play in this drama in which culture is transformed, through contentiousness, into diverse, even divisive, ideologies—which is one dimension of what we call "modernism," or, if you wish, "postmodernism"; the differences, I confess, are still not clear to me. It has the potential to weaken the hegemonic character of culture by revealing the relations between social structure and symbolic structure and, by making those relations visible, to render claims to symbolic consensus debatable and, perhaps, induce some reflexive consciousness of the ways in which one's cultural predispositions are implicated in one's social location—and shaped by it. A determinist sociology of culture, in short, attempts to make visible the grip of what Bourdieu calls "habitus," and by its visibility to enable one to free oneself from it, thereby potentially increasing one's range of conscious choice.

To render habitus (the not necessarily conscious influence of socialization and internalization) visible, then, is not unlike a collective equivalent to the promise of a successful psychoanalysis to free the individual patient from the ignorance of repression. It has that educative, liberational quality. But one must guard against the error of believing that detachment from socialized habit, neurotic or not, is something universally or devoutly to be wished. Despite Yeats's famous lines that the best lack all conviction while the worst are full of passionate intensity, few people are likely to be willing to risk yielding the certainty of their convictions or the "naturalness" of their feelings to the relativisms of sociological analysis. What Freud knew about the unconscious, Simmel and others knew about socialization: to render it visible is full of mortal risks. It's already more than fifty years since Erich Fromm pointed to the fact that freedom can be an intolerable burden from which some seek escape; along with freedom may go the *déclassement* that T. S. Eliot saw as social pathology and the anomies and alienations that Durkheim clearly envisioned and that conservative thinkers have warned about in their praise of tradition and their caution about change. Stendhal's Julien Sorel is an early and tragic archetype of the insight that marginality can kill you. Let's invoke one of those conservative insights and suggest that no society can endure without some hegemonic culture; without it routine interaction and ordinary civil discourse would be inconceivable. Is it evidence, then, of some inherent tendency to social equilibrium to observe that the transformation of hegemonic culture into diverse ideologies is usually accompanied by an opposite process in which, over time, some ideologies win sufficient allegiance to approach newly hegemonic status (e.g., some minimum "floor" of welfare payments to the deserving poor?), and that some long-established hegemonies remain uncontested?

Nothing I have said so far, however, should be read to mean that the direction of causality has been doctrinally prejudged. What I do take as axiomatic is that any effort at "scientific" thinking should aim at reducing indeterminacy. For sociologists, that means increasing our sociological understanding, and that calls forth a tendency to focus on the impact of social structure on cultural or psychological or other variables in what Randall Collins calls the "chains" of interaction constituting what we actually study. In this tendency sociologists are not different from other "ologists," who usually regard their own axioms and the subject matter they indicate as irreducible fundament, vis-à-vis which other data are epiphenomenal or "dependent." Biologists, economists, psychologists, and so on each tend to emphasize the autonomy or the causal primacy of the data (genetic structure, marginal utility, stimulus-response) whose mastery constitutes their special expertise, "grounding" or "anchoring" (terrestrial or marine metaphors may be variously relevant) the study of what they don't yet understand in terms of what they think they do understand.

17 / AGENCY, DETERMINISM, CHOICE

Dictionaries are ambiguous about "agency." An agent, they tell us, is an instrument, someone who acts for someone else. Sometimes agency is endowed with the power to cause change, as in the action of a "chemical agent," but notice that the chemical action is necessary and predictable, which is no comfort to those for whom "agency" is somehow code for freedom or autonomous power. Am I an "agent" here and now? An agent of what? History? Society? Sociology? Myself? I reproduce *as* an agent, through my willed agency, the form and structure of such occasions as the publication of this small book (and the academic lectures that preceded it) for its probably small audience of readers and reviewers. Functioning as a professor or critical intellectual, I come before you to present my "independent" and "autonomous" thoughts, and you flatter me by kindly keeping your eyes on the page and attending to my words—hoping that you will read something fresh and interesting (or at least not stale and banal). But even in the unlikely event that I give you one of the most trenchant essays on culture you've ever read, what I say will be assimilated to the form of the academic colloquy, and its structure will be reproduced. If I'm good or very good what I say may be discussed for a while; it may even influence some readers—although probably not unless they are structurally predisposed to hear me as an ally rather than as an enemy or a competitor. If I'm very bad that too may preoccupy discussion for more than a while, such discourse, like gossip, thriving as it does on weaknesses rather than strengths. Still, more important than anything extremely interesting or extremely banal that I write here is that the structure of what *we* do here will have been (a rare future perfect tense entirely appropriate to our business of anticipating consequences) reproduced. Of course I can choose to write what I wish (if I have the talent and the resources), but I can't control all the conditions in which it is written and I can't create the environment in which you will hear what I say in the way I want you to hear it. Totalitarian dictators, I am told, to some extent do have that kind of control, which would surely tempt anyone. I read recently vis-à-vis the surrender of communist dictatorships in eastern Europe a pious proclamation to the effect that all tyrannies eventually fall. The proclaimer failed to note the other side of that half-truism: that all benevolent regimes eventually fall too.

I said earlier that I wanted to make a contribution to the reintegration of voluntarism and structuralism (or sociological determinism). I hope you can see by now the outline of the contribution I want to make. Of course people make choices every day in every way. You choose to be reading this today; those who might want to but aren't reading it chose to be otherwise occupied, and both of these choices are made under a series of constraints and incentives set by social structure and more or less legitimated by internalized culture. The business of a generalizing sociology of culture is to understand as exactly as possible how a specific range of possible choices is presented to the consciousness of a potentially active agent, and how situational or intervening variables (i.e., relatively micro-social structures) reinforce or undermine the pre-disposition to choose from among the range of possible choices; a process going from possibility to probability—always with the prospect of a lot of unexplained variance because there are more variables operative in everyday life than any social scientist can take account of, much less control. Sociological understanding is the effort to reduce that unexplained variance, in short to reduce indeterminacy. And for me that's what has made sociology interesting—and demonic—for the forty years I have been involved with it. In *Lord Jim*, Joseph Conrad (one of my favorite sociologists) has a character named Stein tell the anguished Jim (anguished by his cowardice and resolved to redeem himself): "In the destructive element immerse." (Stein's a German, verbs at the end.) There's no more destructive element for a liberal believer in freedom than sociology; it will really test you. That, perhaps, is the metaphysical pathos in my own work, although it may be bad form for me to say so; judgments about one's own metaphysical pathos are better left to others.

One of my students, Perry Deess, says that the sociologist Bill Sewell can't abide an "agentless determinism," and that research must "look beyond" material and structural conditions. But look where? The line of sight leads either to a compromised idealism or to seeing "agency" as a problem that structures must solve. In structuralist (or nonconstitutive) theories, it is said, "People keep getting society done to them, rather than doing it themselves." A good sentence; but it still retains the old (and often false) antinomy between structure and agency. The point is not whether they do it or get it done to them; like Willis's lads, they always do it themselves but usually in ways that promote it being done to them; like the "possession" of culture, we don't have it unless it has us—not either/or but both/and. In Willis's work we see agency married to structure, agency as *part* of structure-as-practice. Yes, surely, that's a determinist formulation, but a determinism with so many still-mysterious variables at work that, in effect, agents may still feel free. Harold Garfinkel (1967) was surely at least partly right when he said that people are not "cultural dopes" (though there may have been a bit of ideological pandering in the observation; flattered readers will be predisposed to think you right), but it does not follow that they always know the meaning of what they do.

Now if this image of more or less probabilistically determined individual choosers offends you, don't cry reductionism or oversimplification and moan about deterministic efforts to reduce human complexity. Look for sustenance to the people who fall into the categories of unexplained variance, and who therefore may be regarded as having outwitted—at least so far—the voracity of social structure. On the other hand, if you're marketing products or political candidates, you'd probably want the indeterminacy reduced as much as possible to maximize predictable markets and minimize risk or bottom-line loss. But if you're a believer in freedom and contingency and evasion and recalcitrance (I resist therefore I am, as Alvin Gouldner once put it), then you'd probably want to increase the amount of unexplained variance; you'd want, in a sense, to defeat sociology, and so another contribution I'd like to make to this debate is to invoke Georg Simmel, who in effect told us how.

As a phrase, "the complexity of everyday life" evokes for me what all ethnographers and depth interviewers know but must neglect under the exigencies of writing a coherent and inevitably selective research report: that life is simultaneously more subtle and more gross, more poignant and more banal, duller and more exciting, nobler and more base, more terrifying and more glorious than any social science rendering of it is likely to be. We may know a good bit about the ways in which ("other things being equal") the interaction of age, income, race, ethnicity, occupation, gender, education, and other major variables function to produce structures of power, preference, constraint, and incentive. But other things are seldom equal, there are surely a large number of other variables operative in everyday life, and small interactive differences among them can produce very large unanticipated consequences—as, for example, chaos theory has persuasively suggested and as the collapse of the East German regime (without any visibly strong movements of dissent preceding it) and other recent events in eastern Europe indicate.

Everyday life, then, is full of both order and unexpected turns, as well as other surprises. Simmel understood this, and so did the Chicago "symbolic interactionists," who learned it—if not exactly from him then ultimately through him. In reacting against structural or "mechanical" explanations of cultural practice, some symbolic interactionists may have gone too far in implying that practice could be fully understood without going beyond the situation of micro-interaction itself. Goffman, on the other hand, despite his almost exclusive focus on micro-situations, understood that macro-structures create *conditions of interaction* that contain their own micro-structures. By opposing "interaction" to "structure," some symbolic interactionists revealed a metaphysical pathos that burdened interaction (as distinguished from "mechanical" relations) with the deus ex machina-like role of producing—presto—innovation, creativity and so on, whereas most real interaction is routine and predictable, founded as it is on our abilities accurately to "take the role" of another.

Simmel, however, taught us that even the most sociologistic of sociologies could still accommodate a concept of the elusive "individual" if only because no two persons have exactly the same set of social memberships; no two persons have been subject to exactly the same processes of socialization; no biography is identical to that of any other. Therefore every person, in a strictly sociological sense, is in some respects unique, and that is one theoretical mode of understanding the empirical inevitability of some unexplained variance or individuality without mystifying the inner life.

But how do we tap this uniqueness? How do we nudge or encourage the "individuals" perhaps struggling to break free from the role players they inhabit? Think of it this way: if we like and admire unique and "individual" people (but remember that we don't always; some believe there's too much emphasis on being individual or unique and not enough on communal proprieties) because they are "interesting," what we usually mean is that their behavior and ideas are fresh, unusual, arresting, even unpredictable. For me, for example, "independent" thinkers are those for whom I find it difficult to infer what they're likely to think or do about A from my previous knowledge of what they thought or did about B and C. Most people's views come in packages that can be labeled according to the particular consistencies that characterize them—although specific patterns of consistency may be difficult to discover. David Riesman has always seemed to me a highly independent thinker (unlike other major thinkers who spawn a generation of disciples and hence risk becoming prisoners of their own "schools of thought") precisely because his views on any specific issue were hard to predict. It was almost as if he felt obliged to think every important issue through to a reasoned conclusion, unlike most of the rest of us who may not have the time, energy, or inclination for that, and hence rely on our reference groups to provide us with most of our "received" ideas. I can't say, for example, that I have ever really thought through the merits of Saving the Whales or the arguments for and against the Strategic Defense Initiative (Star Wars), but I'm for saving the whales and against Star Wars because "my people," the folks I identify myself with, are for the whales and against Star Wars. Is that an instance of "political correctness"? If so, I confess willingly to it, but would remind you that we all have a tendency toward political correctness, particularly concerning issues that we have not had the time or inclination to think through "independently."

If "interesting" people are those who are *relatively* unpredictable (not so unpredictable as to approach insanity) how did they get to be that way? My hypothesis, admittedly a reductionist one, is that interesting people (more often than uninteresting people) have social biographies that have packaged their identities in unusual ways. Years ago Malcolm Cowley reported on an informal survey of American poets. Most of them, he said, apparently suffered from some infirmity in childhood that impeded them from being like other kids (the wound and the bow theme again). Similarly, mixed marriage, religious crisis or change, international migration or other kinds of mobility that destabilize social relations, irregular generational placement in families create unusual patterns of intersection in Simmelian social circles, and hence unusually complex identities. Rose Laub Coser goes further than Simmel to suggest that the more complex one's personal history of group membership, the more complex one's culture and hence one's thinking. This is in principle a quantitative conception, with no doubt a lot of still unexplained variance. Craziness sometimes results from social memberships *too* complex to integrate; too much complexity or instability, like too little, may lead people to opt for predictably rigid doctrines. Still, the generalization may hold despite these exceptions at the margins.

So if you want to maintain a lot of unexplained variance or indeterminacy (and remember: not everyone does, and no one *always* does) and hence sustain your image of human beings as free and autonomous agents, while at the same time not sacrificing your sociological understanding of such matters, try to create social arrangements that foster bundles of identities that are not so predictably packaged. Oppose the glorification of deep and lasting "commitments to community," and encourage relatively shallow and contingent attachments to communities—to a lot of them, diverse and heterogeneous, in which the depth and contingency of one's memberships/attachments are variable. Cast a jaded eye on the celebration of loyalty or fidelity *as* abstraction and *to* abstractions; ask instead: loyalty to what? fidelity to whom? Cultivate those odd social niches whose resources enable you to claim the voice of a "member" but that also provide alternative resources for effective dissent and resistance. Every community exacts some degree of conformity or compliance as its price of membership, and this is not necessarily felt as constraint, particularly if the community's rules and norms are one's own, and especially if one has never even had the occasion to think consciously about them. Plural and diverse memberships constitute conditions that make it increasingly *vital* to think about them and, as Rose Coser (1991) points out, to interact with diverse significant others regarding what to do about possibly contradictory signals from one's different reference groups, or conflicting pressures or commands from different authorities. The need to mull over such problems is generated by plural and diverse memberships that increase the prospect of being reflexive about one's own socialization, and therefore can increase one's discretionary powers. If you want to be free, in short, don't put all your identity eggs in one basket; the best strategy for your cultural assets is, as stockbrokers say about financial assets, diversify.

Not everyone wants to be free in that sense, of course. "Commitment" has long had cultural status as a virtue, and most people probably feel most free when their socialized commitments are unreflexive, that is, "natural." Reflexiveness, as I have said, is not something usually devoutly to be wished, "sicklied o'er," as it is, "by the pale cast of thought." Hamlet knew at first hand the anguish, even the paralysis of ambivalence between revenging his father and the constraints exercised by his position in the Danish court. There are plenty of risks in reflexivity; it may even constitute a bizarre dystopian image. But it is as close as most of us will ever get to a sociological sense of freedom.

Historically speaking, however, sociology has not always had this jaded take on freedom; its meanings too are contextual. In the 1920s social and cultural determinism was projected (and received) as a liberation from the tyranny of biological imperatives; culture, it was successfully argued (and eventually supported with research), could shape, modify, and mould "instincts." By the 1950s and 1960s its success was complete; so much so that the perception of enslavement to biology was replaced by the perception of enslavement to culture and socialization, and "freedom" was sought in the unconscious, to be revealed by psychoanalysis (Trilling 1951, Wrong 1961), drugs, or Eastern meditative techniques or other monkish disciplines. Simmel, with his strictly sociological account of individuality, showed us a way out of this historical oscillation, and Bourdieu's materialist reflexivity renders individuality as a purely empirical question, a matter of the interaction of "habitus" and "field," and the resources in cultural capital they provide. If, as Bourdieu suggests (following Durkheim), mental schemata are "nothing other" than the embodiment of social divisions (an adequate social science, he says, must encompass objective regularities *and* the processes of socialization that constitute them), how is it that scholars, artists, and others strive for "creativity" and "originality?" Well, like "commitment," creativity and originality have long had good cultural press; hence there's a lot less creativity and originality than there are people wanting to be "creative" and "original." Moreover, strictly speaking, most artists and intellectuals don't strive for originality, or don't in any purely abstract sense; John Kenneth Galbraith's phrase "permissible originality" comes to mind here. There are more or less strict rules and conventions that govern every genre in which "creative" people work, and they usually work within and around those rules and conventions. Robert Frost, in a famous remark, expressed his disdain of unrhymed free verse, which he likened to "playing tennis without a net." Frost lost that particular argument, and innovations of course occur in poetry and other arts, as well as in other regions of culture "creative" and not. But the originalities are permissible ones, or are eventually seen as permissible additions to or changes in a tradition by communities that warrant or certify the innovation as "creative" or "original" rather than as crazy, unintelligible, or incoherent. A typical problem of an avant-garde in any region of culture is to persuade the relevant "field" that the avant-garde's work represents an important advance in the accumulated tradition of that field or a significant departure from it that must nevertheless be respected. Ideological work is eternal.

18 / INSTITUTIONAL DOMINANCE

Still, it is easy to forget that the "economic," the "political," the "cultural," and so on are abstractions whose causal salience may be variable, relative to (1) the objective differentiation of institutional structures and (2) which institution actually dominates the life of a society at a given time and place, and against what opposition. As Sahlins points out (and as others have both before and after him), Marxist analysis of base-superstructure relations, in which causality goes primarily from the economy (base) to other institutional sectors (superstructure), is simply not relevant in "primitive" societies that are not institutionally differentiated; where, for example, economy and kinship and polity and law are not *separate* organizational structures, and may be vested in the same persons and groups, and where kinship is likely to be the dominant institution. Even without institutional differentiation, however, the separate *functions* can be differentiated and their relations analyzed for the tensions and complementarities they generate.

To say that institutional dominance is located in the economy in highly differentiated advanced capitalist societies may have several meanings relevant in this context. For example, it means that very large profit-seeking enterprises are increasingly decisive in nonprofit sectors of society—say, in the structure of family life or the viability of a small political community after a plant closing. It also means that economic values (efficiency, scale, "bottom-line mentalities") become increasingly pervasive in nonprofit organizations. That pervasiveness is evident, for example, in the wide use of cost-benefit reasoning even in those circumstances where costs and benefits are not clearly calculable in any bottom-line terms, in the waxing of "rational-choice" theorizing, and, perhaps most importantly, in the conceptual transformation of cohorts, publics, audiences, and constituencies (collectivities from which "political" and "cultural" organizations seek support) into "markets" (collectivities from which "economic" organizations seek support).

It's worth noting here that although economic (i.e., profit-seeking) organizations typically create and carry more or less distinctive minicultures (customs, values, symbols, style—e.g., the distinctive "corporate cultures" of, say, General Motors or IBM), in common usage we usually reserve the term "cultural organization" to enterprises such as ballet, opera, and theater companies, symphony orchestras, museums (art), libraries, universities, labs, think tanks (knowledge), local historical societies, fraternal associations (solidarity), and churches (morality). We do this in part, of course, as an expression of the association of most of these activities with the tradition of elite cultivation mentioned earlier in this essay; but we also do it *because* they are not usually profit-seeking (or at least not often profit-making) activities, and hence must be subsidized as "causes" worthy of public or private (or both) philanthropic support, depending on whether their worthiness is a matter of national cultural consensus or merely a matter of noblesse oblige or other sectoral ideal interests. But note too that when cultural organizations *do* become profit-making (as in professional sports, film, television, publishing, journalism, advertising, pop music), we have to be reminded from time to time, in order to keep our priorities straight, that these are industries, businesses governed less by the pursuit of the self-evidently worthy (the true, the beautiful, the good) than by what their respective markets will bear. In its more extreme and aggressive form the argument is sometimes made that the self-evidently worthy is in fact nothing more than what the markets for truth, beauty, and goodness will bear: never tell more truth than your markets can bear to hear.

Indeed, where economic institutions are dominant, the transformation of publics into markets (or the market character of publics) becomes increasingly taken for granted and hegemonic. As that occurs, insistence on the autonomy or the self-evident value of what cultural organizations seek (art, knowledge, moral integrity, or, for that matter, community—in recent years, say, the threatened life-style associated with the family farm) seems increasingly sentimental or arbitrary, nostalgic, "unrealistic," and sometimes even relegated to that sector of opinion called the lunatic fringe.

Finally, institutional dominance (whether it be multinational conglomerates, the Party in formerly communist countries, the Church in the European Middle Ages, or military regimes) is an effort to neutralize the autonomous differentiation of institutions (central to theorizing about "civil society" and the evolution from the primitive to the modern) and hence to dominate a complex society in ways analogous to those in which kinship is said to preside over simpler societies.

The efforts of dominant institutions, however, are seldom unopposed. It is easy for sociologists to forget that institutional abstractions only metaphorically carry action in social life. Action is ultimately carried by persons, more or less organized groups pursuing proximate aims in circumstances whose built-in incentives may facilitate the pursuit, who may also have to cope with abstract institutional ("political," "legal," "economic," "familial," and so on) constraints and overt opposition from other persons and groups differently situated. The very dynamism of societies in which economic institutions are dominant creates uneven rates of change in different sectors, uproots populations, generates mal-integration, weakens traditions in ways beneficial to some but injurious to others. It creates motivated opposition. Hence at any given historical moment and in any context of mutual push and shove, the direction of causality is not necessarily given by theoretical doctrines which, like that of Marx and Engels, see an economic base determining a cultural superstructure (though conservative parties typically praise free markets and deregulation while deploring their cultural impact on families), or, like that of Sahlins, see the causality reversed, but by the empirical balance of material and ideal resources and constraints affecting the relevant actors. The weight of those resources and constraints varies by time and place.

Is all this merely temporizing in behalf of moderation or "multi-dimensionality?" What's the point here? Is it that economic institutions are not reliably causal? No, it's that, though institutional dominance varies, the economic is virtually never negligible. The recent tendency of theorists to impute "relative autonomy" to the realm of culture is perhaps even more misleading than the tendency to see the institutional dominance of, say, corporate money as irresistible. All the empirical problems of "relative autonomy" come down to questions of *how* autonomous? for how long? and relative to what? Every milieu worthy of the name provides its participants with some set of resources (from piddling to powerful) not only for the pursuit of their aims but for resisting the efforts of others to determine or dominate their lives. Such autonomy depends on the effectiveness of resources (including the ability to mobilize them) relative to the mobilized resources of opposed others intent upon reducing or controlling the autonomy claimed. In any long-run conflict between principles (as pieces of culture) and material interests, the interests usually prevail—although it may take some time to formulate the ideological work necessary to rationalize alterations in the principles so that new courses of action or policies may be legitimated by them. In the process, of course, some people may be willing to die for their principles and beliefs and may be posthumously praised as heroes. But, in the nature of the case, there are few enough heroes (no offense intended to Oskar Schindler, or the larger-than-life Willy Loman, or all the unsung bravery of everyday life), and as the principles become modified, heroism may seem to some increasingly reckless or imprudent.

19 / RESISTANCE THEORY

"Resistance theory," for example, has often been invoked by neo-Marxists over the past decade in behalf of the efforts by subordinate groups to use the resources of their subcultures to oppose (or "resist") efforts by a dominant institution to impose its hegemonic culture on them (Willis 1981; Lipsitz 1990; Giroux 1981; Foley 1990). Lost, however, in the efforts by these scholars to celebrate resistance as active "agency" is the fact that the resistance is seldom very effective; resisters resist, all right, but the resistance is usually either defeated or produces ironic consequences that reproduce the very system of domination-subordination they seem to be resisting.

The question of whether causal analysis concludes with optimism or pessimism about the prospects of reducing inequality is a decisive criterion for resistance theory and its partisans in choosing whether to accept or reject the analysis—almost as if the scholar were obliged to see "active agency" and resistance (for example by working-class students against the dominant culture of the school) as grounds for hopeful assertions about the autonomy of the schoolboys in striking a blow against the middle-class hegemony of the school. Academic "objectivity," of course, constrains scholars to ignore optimism and pessimism as cognitively irrelevant to the viability of empirical conclusions: its command is to go where the evidence leads. Weber's gloom about the iron cage may motivate those depressed by it to find some escape from functional rationality and the inevitabilism of bureaucratic routine. But the evidence, not the gloom, is the legitimate object of critique—although the gloom may motivate the critique. Althusser (1972), Bowles and Gintis (1976), and Bourdieu (with Passeron 1977) are favorite targets of "resistance theory" because of their bleak visions of the endless reproduction of inequality (in schools and elsewhere), apparently incorrigible short of something like a revolution, and perhaps not even then. Such conclusions are criticized less for their failures of evidence or logic than, of all things, for their pessimism, one important aspect of which is "reducing" human actors to passive role players who simply "reflect" the structural constraints imposed on them, from the macro-structures that define the limits of their range of choice to the micro-structures (or situational variables) that affect their predisposition to choose among the options available to them.

Willis's book is important not because he shows us how culture is autonomous or how working-class boys reproduce inequality by choosing their futures (rather than having it forced upon them). It's important because it's poignant and almost epically tragic to see how all that sassy energy and vitality come to naught; how the comforts of working-class culture are small compensation for the structurally limited horizons the boys face. Willis can't promise them anything better. Despite Willis's efforts to avoid it, the conclusion to be drawn from his own evidence is that it doesn't seem to make much difference whether you're an active resister or a passive acquiescent or, for that matter (filling out the implicit fourfold table) a passive resister or an active acquiescent. When flies get stuck on flypaper are their efforts to flutter free evidence of struggle and resistance or merely part of a scripted ritual of death in which the desperate strength-sapping efforts are part of the script? The pessimist will breathe a melancholy "aaahh"; the optimist will shout "people are not flies!" The optimist will point to the few who perhaps escape; the pessimist to the many who don't. (Of course if it's *your* fly-paper in *your* kitchen, you may see more escaping than permanently stuck, and you may be gloomy about that.) The researcher will try to control the intervening variables to discover the conditions predicting the different outcomes.

Still, the optimist is quite correct; people, of course, are not flies. But they do seem like relatively passive role players much of the time; it's what we call social order and are grateful for it more often than not. And Paul Willis's working-class boys resist the culture of the school in role, *as* working-class boys. Relative autonomy? Active agency? These may reproduce the structure of domination and subordination as often as they undermine it. It might ironically amuse resistance theorists to understand that in rejecting pessimism out of hand they are affirming a piece of the dominant culture that derogates "gloom and doom sayers," preferring thumbs that are up, faces that are smiling, sentences that begin "Hopefully . . .", and spirits eager for the next challenge.

One should not underestimate the cultural resonance represented by images of resistance to (or eventual compliance with) the blunt power exercised by rationally structured (though perhaps not yet fully legitimated) social forces. One of the major appeals of science fiction as a genre of popular culture is its convention of projecting into the future (far or near) current rationalizing trends and the incipient possibilities they represent for conflict with traditional culture, where heroes resist illegitimate force. There was a prescient film called *Rollerball* (1975) that contained a pair of incisive metaphors sufficient to carry the entire film. Set in the near future, the movie portrays multinational corporations as having replaced nation-states (too violently confrontational, too unstable for good business) as the major administrative (there is no public politics) units of populations. Their managing directors provide a version of bread and circuses, peace and prosperity to all, but they also provide violent amusements to their apparently otherwise bored and potentially resistant employees. Guests dressed in evening clothes for a dinner party at an elegant country estate sit out on a terrace aiming lasers at a line of trees, each of which, when hit, bursts into spectacular flames. For more ordinary people the directors also sponsor worldwide competitions in a sport called rollerball, which combines several of the more violent aspects of American football, basketball, hockey, and roller derby competition. The games attract millions of fans to enormous stadiums where they cheer wildly for "their" teams, and star players, naturally, become world-renowned celebrities. But if, as happens in the film, a star player becomes *so* celebrated that he feels free to resist a decision by the managing directors (in this case to "transfer" the star's wife to a VIP claimant on her companionship), the rollerball rules are changed to permit greater and greater violence, producing at first the deaths of some players, and eventually a playing field transformed into a war zone in which, for everyone, the battle is to the death with no rules at all.

The fans love it. The twin metaphors are economic/political domination represented by the cool bureaucratic rationality of the directors, and the cultural power represented by the innocent dedication of the players to the game, and their efforts to cope with the increasing anarchy of the rules. *Rollerball* was a moderately successful Hollywood film, and our recalcitrant hero, of course, is left standing at the end amidst the carnage. George Orwell's hero in *1984* did not prevail; his resistance came to nothing. Orwell's grim pessimism is sustainable in a serious novel, but commercial films prefer their heroes defiant to the end. The movie made of Orwell's book was, not surprisingly, a large commercial failure.

The extreme and contrasting image to the sociological determinism I have been celebrating here is one of free and unpredictable choosers from an unlimited range of options—which would make a social science absurd and impossible. Even with Tocqueville's formulation of "partly determined, partly free" it's difficult even to imagine how one might empirically distinguish "passive role players" from "active agents." The emphasis on one or the other is less an empirical matter than one of metaphysical pathos. Everyone does both (plays roles and makes fateful choices), often simultaneously, but the important thing sociologically is that they do more or less of it, depending on the kinds and amounts of structural constraints they endure, the incentives and opportunities they enjoy, and the cultural capital at their disposal. Yes, we all have choices and are agents of our own destinies. I'm grateful that we have thirty-one choices at Baskin-Robbins and that there are lots of detergents and brands of beer on the grocery store shelf. But meta-choices count too, and I don't remember getting the opportunity to choose whether I wanted that many choices among ice creams, beers, and detergents. Freedom of choice is increasingly framed, in the U.S. at least, as *consumer* choice. I don't get to make nearly as many producer choices as I'd like because these are mostly private (not public) decisions jealously guarded by the powerful persons who make them. I'd like more choice among viable political candidates than I'm likely to get in the next election. But I'm not likely to get the opportunity to make that meta-choice for reasons largely explainable in macro-structural terms.

20 / THE RELATIVE AUTONOMY OF CULTURE

Although above I have defended efforts at reductionism in behalf of reducing indeterminacy, nothing in this essay is intended to suggest that culture, ideology, or consciousness *must* be reduced to "objective" economic interests. There is no good reason to doubt that at some times, in some places, under some conditions, culture and ideology (as well as their subjectively felt equivalents: belief, taste, emotion) have been or may be causally powerful in affecting "political" or "economic" events (Bell 1976; Bellah 1988; Mukerji 1989; Thompson 1964; Collins 1981; Sahlins 1976; Douglas 1969; Schudson 1989)—particularly where the events at issue tap deeply held cultural assumptions that are threatened by those issues, and hence evoke strong moral, aesthetic, or religious feeling, as is the case, for example, with abortion and with art described as obscene, blasphemous, or otherwise morally offensive. Religion is perhaps the strongest example of symbolic meanings exercising causal force in public and private life. Note, however, that in the modern world religious fervor is probably least strong in elite congregations whose ties to the material world are most complex, whereas ecstatic or otherwise passionate religious feeling in the West tends to be associated with mostly self-contained sects or cults.

The autonomy of a piece of culture seems strongest when it is most hegemonic, taken for granted, or when the evolution of "culture" toward "ideology" is in its early stages. The causal salience of the "cultural" or of some other analytic dimension depends also on at what point you cut into the chain of events with your investigation. The point, however, is that, abstracted as "ideal interests," culturally shaped feelings are likely to seem "purely" ideal; in fact they tend to be interpenetrated with material interests as well, and when they are, their *cultural* intensity is enhanced (Luker 1984; witness the NEA controversy).

Let me be clear: I am not suggesting that at any given moment of historical time cultural (symbolic) variables don't have some independent effects; plainly they sometimes do. Some people some of the time express and act on beliefs and principles apparently unaccountable in terms of social structure. But statistically they seem to be relatively few, and of those few more than occasionally bizarre. The events at the Branch Davidian compound in Waco, Texas, and the events at the People's Temple commune at Jonestown, Guyana, come to mind as extreme examples of "principled" cultural resistance to pressures from outside. Note, however, that in cases like these, where we disapprove of the particular principles (or regard their implementation as crazy, bizarre, fanatic), pundits do not hesitate to indulge a kind of coarse sociological or social-psychological vocabulary to explain the "purity" of the come-what-may devotion of cult members to their beliefs. We speak of "brainwashing," of "charismatic" leaders, and we construct (usually pathological) social profiles of the types of people most susceptible to brainwashing by particular kinds of charisma. If these aren't enough we look for material conditions and physical threats to understand how the faithful are kept in line.

Even in less extreme instances of symbolic factors having apparently "independent" causal force, they are seldom random. Those of us who work in the major symbolic realms (particularly nonprofit ones) may be driven by ideal interests as much as, sometimes more than, by material interests. We *expect* clergymen, teachers, artists, and scientists to be morally, aesthetically, or cognitively more pure than the rest of us, and when they aren't, the disapproval is likely to be more severe. Moreover, the extreme "moralism" of some youth is something that many adults expect (even hope) they will "grow out of" as they become more embedded in families, careers, and communities. Such reductionisms comfort us. Many would be offended rather than comforted, however, if what David Bloor calls a "symmetrical" mode of analysis (i.e., the same "reductive" one used to understand Jim Jones's and David Koresh's people) were applied to the heroes and heroines whose devotion to revered symbolic principles was similarly recalcitrant to practical pressures for "reasonable" compromise (Joan of Arc, Nathan Hale, protectors of Jews under Nazi occupation, etc.). In the sociology of science, then, David Bloor thinks that the same mode of analysis should be applied to truth as to error; in the sociology of culture the same mode of analysis should be applied whether we approve or disapprove of the culture in question.

Religion and nationalism/patriotism probably constitute the most powerful examples of culture exercising apparently independent symbolic force. Too much blood has been spilled over the years in their name to treat their cultural claims lightly. Yet theology is always constrained to some extent by churches, the character of their organization, and their constituencies. The Catholic Church in the U.S., for example, is beset with conflicts generated by the resistance of some of its members to official church policies on contraception, abortion, and priestly celibacy, and by dissident members of the priesthood. That these constitute organizational and political problems for the Church (rather than purely cultural ones) is indicated by its reluctance to resort to extreme symbolic sanctions like excommunication; indeed, by its ambivalent tendency to look the other way—a practice so typical in a wide variety of circumstances where official norms generate widespread deviance from them that sociologists have devised a *concept* to describe the general practice: *institutionalized* evasion of rules, in which official institutions themselves are complicit in supporting or tolerating deviance from or evasion of their own rules. These complicities occur most often in circumstances where strict enforcement of legal or cultural rules would create deep conflict or other practical problems that, it is believed, prudence dictates we avoid. The examples are endless, and include such practices as plea bargaining, suspended sentences, the availability of liquor in officially "dry" jurisdictions, and "arranged" evidence of adultery in the days when that was the sole legal ground for divorce.

When religion is combined with nationalism or patriotism, of course, the cultural force generated may be enormous: Pakistan and India; Palestinians and Israelis; Serbia, Croatia, and Bosnia; Northern Ireland. Yet even in the face of the power of such "isms," efforts to understand their power can be obstructed by mystifying the passions they represent as elemental or primordial forces. Close examination of such instances will usually reveal that there are leaders and other prominent persons who have a lot to gain, materially speaking, by stirring religious or nationalist feeling, and peasant or working-class followers without a lot to lose by responding to or otherwise indulging the religious or nationalist passions proffered by those identities. It is important, for example, that Islamic fundamentalisms often represent resistance to Westernization (which has brought little if any material benefits to peasant populations) and insist not only on compliance with a particular interpretation of sacred rules and practices but on the establishment of theocracies in which civil law must yield to sacred commands—but also to leaders who, in administering a state, must be mindful of (if not exclusively beholden to) its material interests.

These remarks, of course, do not constitute new insights. I make them, though, less for their substantive relevance than for the methodological strictures they imply for the study of culture. Are religion and nationalism "relatively autonomous" as culturally causal forces? They surely seem to be. But this does not mean that it is illuminating to speak as if culture "did" something. Ask not what your country can do for you; don't even ask what you can do for your country; ask, rather, who invokes country (or religion or nation or family—or any revered abstract loyalty)? under what conditions? to what ends? with what consequences? Will such questions weaken commitment, dampen the fire of passion? They might; but probably mostly among those "worst" described by Yeats as "full of passionate intensity" and disdained by Weber for their ethic of ultimate ends. On the other hand, satisfactory answers to those questions can sustain, even strengthen, religious, national, or other moral feelings or identities without exacting high costs in rational reflection.

Michael Schudson is a partisan, for example, of the causal efficacy of culture. Recognizing that culture does not *always* "work," he makes a useful contribution by formulating, with his "5 R's," the conditions under which it is likely to work, that is, when a piece of culture has retrievability, rhetorical force, resonance, institutional retention, and resolution. But even when a piece of culture meets some or all of these conditions, is it "the culture" that is causally effective or an interest-guided decision by persons or groups to *invoke* the culture at a specific time and place for their own self-interested purposes (which may then initiate discussions in which different "interested" parties participate)? I prefer the latter formulation because it involves live bodies doing things that can be studied empirically. Former Senator Gary Hart was forced out of the 1988 presidential primaries by revelations of his adulteries, and similar charges threatened Bill Clinton's candidacy in 1992. As a widely shared moral vice, adultery is surely a piece of culture. But "widely shared" has a nice double entendre in this context: widely believed to be a vice indicative of flawed character, but also widely practiced—by some estimates upward of 50 percent of married men commit adultery, with married women not very far behind. Culture begins to weaken when its rules and conventions are ignored with impunity. The next step in the evolution of culture toward ideology is the invention of arguments defending the propriety of deviance.

Another, more homely, example of how material and ideal interests connect in ways that reveal the relativeness of the "relative autonomy" of culture: thirty years ago coed dormitories in college were unthinkable, and a young woman could be routinely expelled for cohabiting with her boyfriend or fiancé (the men, of course, were not usually punished). Today, of course, coed dorms and cohabitation are unremarkable, the results of gradual and relatively quiet changes in cultural norms (abetted by technological innovations in birth control) that evoked little opposition in California, and not much more elsewhere. Abortion, on the other hand, continues to polarize the nation. How is it that these two issues, both presumably (and deeply) "about" the culture of sexuality had such extremely different outcomes? In seeking an answer, I would ask what *material* interests are implicated in these distinctively cultural conflicts. The rules once observed in loco parentis by colleges and universities (still observed on some campuses) were designed to protect the "virtue" (i.e., virginity) of young women. But the virtue of virginity was directly linked to the marriageability of young females, in which they *and* their parents had a clear *material* interest; the old culture "said" men wanted to marry virgins; nonvirgins were, as the once extant terminology had it, "ruined," "damaged goods," whose value in the marriage market was severely diminished. When that linkage between ideal and material interest was broken (i.e., when men started marrying their slept-with lovers in large numbers), virginity-as-cultural-virtue was gradually, and eventually severely, weakened, even positively *de*valued (today, many regard the desire for an utterly inexperienced lover as just a bit kinky), and major political confrontations (hardly now worth the effort) could be avoided.

On the other hand, "pro-life" and "pro-choice" arguments on the abortion controversy, which express ideal interests in the sanctity of life or the freedom to choose, are still directly linked not only to quite different styles of life but to the different material interests that sustain them, and which Kristin Luker has described in detail.

But what, then, about the controversy over homosexuals in the military that dominated political discussion for months in 1993? That's a more complex matter than abortion or premarital chastity or adultery. Feelings about homosexuality are surely a piece of culture, but one of those pieces undergoing a process of change. A generation or two back the cultural consensus was broad that it was disgusting, an unspeakable secret best kept in dark closets. Today it is a matter of ideology about which citizens may disagree—although one of the disagreements is about how legitimate the disagreement itself is (a measure of the relatively early stage of its evolution). Surely, anti-gay sentiment is still sufficiently strong for military authorities to have mounted a purely moral (cultural) argument against sanctioning homosexuality by permitting homosexuals the honor and privilege of serving openly in the armed forces. But they did not make that moral argument (although some may have wanted to); instead they invoked practical, material considerations about their responsibility for the effectiveness of military units as fighting forces, which, they assumed, would be undermined by open homosexuality, an argument that connects the moral issue to the practical issue, the matter of culture to the matter of interests. If the issue is the fitness of fighting forces (rather than one of moral credentials) it is posed as an in-principle empirical issue to which evidence is relevant, even if not much of it was presented. Unmentioned in the debate, however, was the theory of "total institutions," which regards the prospect of intimate exclusive coupling as a source of threat to the single-minded devotion to task and command demanded by the military (Coser 1974; Kanter 1972; Slater 1966). Hence the preference in the military under conditions of battle for either celibacy or utter promiscuity, neither of which generates lasting intimate ties that could compromise exclusive loyalty to the military tasks at hand.

Note, however, that none of these considerations solves the theoretical puzzle of long run-short run directions of causality between base and superstructure, economy and culture, material and ideal interests. The theoretical questions remain "merely" theoretical questions that research (even the best historical studies covering long time frames and comparative cases) is not likely to resolve conclusively. The culture/social structure distinction is of course an "analytic" distinction; individual or group behavior and their legitimations often occur simultaneously and, as we say, "interpenetrate" (a properly erotic term) each other. Nor does it bother me a great deal that the distinction ultimately breaks down; "social structure," like culture, is, after all, an idea. This logical difficulty is what I like to call "merely" theoretical—"merely" because between the analytic distinction and its ultimate breakdown there is a great deal of research space for *empirical* discoveries about the relationships between the behavior of persons constrained by the limits and incentives of their embeddedness in social structures, and the capacity of available and accessible culture and ideologies to provide and sustain legitimations of the behavior.

Though it's not likely to resolve the theoretical question conclusively, what such research can do is attend to the specific linkages between the course of events and reified analytic dimensions of those events that we call the economic, the cultural, the political, and so on. In short, nothing in this essay should encourage students of culture to assume that symbolic meanings can be fully understood by analysis of their inherent formal properties or their eternal character. This is not to say that culture doesn't have formal properties or staying power. Indeed we *need* formal analysis in order to know *what* the culture is that we want to explain—which is one reason why interpretive work on symbolic materials is important. It is to say only that the great bulk of cultural forms, like all human invention, may over time become moribund and has in fact been subject to attenuation or consignment to historical oblivion, as the social arrangements that sustained their vitality were altered by the usual processes of major social change: demographic imbalance or catastrophe, technological innovation, economic crisis, and war.

21 / CULTURE AND PUBLIC POLICY

It's difficult to approach the question of public policy about culture innocently. Given what I have said about culture and ideology, academic assertions about culture and public policy will, like other assertions, properly seem an ideology that serves the interests of the scholars who assert them. The "need" for "more research," *any* research, is one of those academic pieties that deserves a stifled laugh behind the hand. Any claim to serve the public interest must reach for values that concern Americans far beyond the narrow confines of the academic community, which can almost always be counted on to support more research—for reasons having to do with its own material and ideal interests.

Because *legitimate* controversy about culture increasingly characterizes pluralist democracies, and because such controversy is evident in virtually all institutional sectors of such societies (in families, schools, business, churches, the military, mass media, and other institutions of art and entertainment), it is a matter of the public interest that public policy concern itself with the continual *discovery* (rather than the doctrinal proclamation) of the common values that frame the legitimacy of controversy and limit the potential of a Hobbesian war of all against all. Correspondingly, public policy should be concerned with discovering and monitoring the actual extent of subcultural variation (culture wars), and with searching for new sources and modes of negotiating the inevitable conflicts generated by the very legitimacy of ideological diversity within a frame of broadly shared culture.

That last phrase is crucial. A "broadly shared culture" defines, in a sense, the limits beyond which subcultural variation threatens the very conception of a common public life; a definition of what is beyond the pale of public discussion. This is a way of saying that what Gramsci said of bourgeois culture is true of all cultures: they perform hegemonic functions; they remove certain issues from the realm of the discussable, and they remove certain views about issues from the realm of reasonable or "hearable" opinion; more, they make it difficult, if not impossible, even to think about such matters. One of the earliest books about the prospect of nuclear holocaust was called *Thinking about the Unthinkable* (Kahn), a title suggesting that even thinking about nuclear war required breaking through the hegemonic prohibitions on rational public discourse about it. Pluralist democracies are faced with the continued prospect of such breakthroughs by virtue of the very liberties we cherish.

The breakthroughs occur, of course, although not without difficulty. Not long ago, for example, divorce carried with it not only a severe social stigma but was regularly represented by chapters in textbooks on social problems (along with other old reliables like poverty, crime, delinquency, alcoholism, addiction, and so on). That divorce was a "social problem" was a fairly well established "fact" of culture. That is no longer true; it is, in any case, seldom represented in current textbooks on social problems. Still, it remains difficult to invoke the language of "divorce rates" (or, better, "high divorce rates") without knitted brows, pursed lips, or other body language conveying that we're talking about something collectively undesirable. Almost in the sense that Robert Michels identified organization with oligarchy, "high divorce rates" still implies "problem." The *language* remains hegemonic even after the facts of divorce have become relatively normalized—so much so that if one wished to refer neutrally, or even favorably, to the *facts* indicated by the phrase "high divorce rate" (and remarriage) one would face the strong temptation to abandon the conventional language altogether, and substitute new phrases like "shorter marriages" and/or "more frequent marriages." (Euphemism is in the ear of the listener.) And if one wished to do ideological work in behalf of high divorce rates one might argue that shorter and more frequent marriages increase the net amount and variety of experienced intimacy in a population, and may even create additional skills in the management of interpersonal relations.

Similarly, a phrase like "teenage pregnancy" is already established in the common language as a term conveying a judgment of pathology despite the purely descriptive reference it contains, and despite the utterly normal fecundity of human females in their teen years. The "problem," the pathology is neither age nor fertility (the facts the phrase overtly contains) but (1) sexual activity regarded by many as precocious; (2) that most of the pregnant teenagers are unmarried; (3) that many of them, if not most, are poor and/or from ethnic minorities; and (4) that they are therefore a burden to the welfare system (i.e., to us). The linguistic hegemony of "teenage pregnancy" conveys not only pathology but prescribes for the rest of us a peculiar posture of sympathetic concern for the foreclosed futures of such young women (terminated education, for example) mixed with some anger/hostility toward them based on the financial drain they represent and on an image of them as promiscuous.

Looked at from their point of view, however, becoming pregnant, though surely not the best of imaginable events, may be as good as or better than what is "normally" available to them: prolonged adolescence and, for most, a minimum wage job with few prospects even if they finish high school. Pregnancy means a kind of immediate adulthood; her lover just might marry her; and though he probably won't, he probably will show some interest in the child ("evidence" of his potency), and hence some continued interest in her; she gets a baby—someone to love and who will love her; she gets AFDC to supplement whatever she might earn illegally in the informal cash economy; and there may be an extended kin group to care for the child while she's working (Stack 1974).

None of this, of course, is to argue for more divorce or more teenage pregnancies. It is only to suggest that hegemonies may be overcome in struggles over public policy, and that ideologies may be available to assist in that struggle. But I want to argue something more: that the formulation of public policy (over divorce, teen pregnancy, and other matters that involve the hegemony of language) is better served by debates that challenge that hegemony than by thoughtless compliance with an assumed consensus. There may, of course, be proper limits; some hegemonies remain rightfully unchallenged. There is still no substantial constituency in favor of murder (think, though, of "the final solution" or the Argentine "disappeared" or the Central American death squads), and it is still not quite possible to imagine organizing a public forum to discuss the merits of, say, treason or child molestation. Still, thirty years ago, as I said, coed dorms were unthinkable.

Culture is always changing (as well as reproducing itself), and the breaking of its forms as well as its hegemonies may be minor or major, gradual or sudden, involving relatively few people and only minor interests or many people and vital interests (there's an implicit fourfold table there too). The first exhibition in the U.S. of European modern art outraged sensibilities and created near riots in New York before the First World War. From the very beginnings of "rock" music in the early 1950s, traditional moralists warned against its adversary sensibility and the cultural damage it could do to the young—although similar warnings were heard at the turn of the century about ragtime. Powerful political interests were not on the whole severely threatened. In the nineteenth century, however, the U.S. underwent a debilitating civil war over a major cultural issue directly tied to powerful political and economic interests, and the long hot summers of the late 1960s produced small wars in the streets, again over the convergence of cultural and political/economic interests. "The moment the mores are questioned," said William Graham Sumner, "it is a sign they have lost their authority." Pluralist democracies question the mores and question authority routinely now, and that requires increased attention to the culture "we" still (or newly) share, the diversities "we" still (or newly) honor, but also to the arrangements of social structure that sustain or weaken the shared and the diverse. Hypothesis: where incipient cultural changes (and the conflicts generated over them) do not involve important material interests they tend to "blow over"—opposition weakens in ways that permit the incipience to continue its course from the culture of consensus to the legitimacy of ideological diversity. Where culture *is* closely tied to material interests, movement toward change will generate bitter and prolonged struggles over public policy.

22 / A PROGRAM FOR THE SOCIOLOGY OF CULTURE

The relevance of cultural consensus or ideological pluralism to certain public policy issues is only one of several distinct focuses for a program of research in the sociology of culture. Some of the others are studies of the meanings contained in recurrent ritual practices, which, by transcending many of the ideological divisions in a complex society, probably touch, actually or vicariously, very large portions of a society's population (sometimes great majorities) and are probably reproductive or integrative of a widely shared extant culture. I have in mind highly ceremonialized practices such as the Olympic Games, the Miss America contest, the Super Bowl, Mardi Gras, family homecomings at Christmas or Thanksgiving, the World Series, Fourth of July parades and picnics, high school and college commencements, and so on (MacAloon 1981, 1984; Phillips 1988; Real 1977; Davis 1986). But a sociology of these must go beyond an analysis of their meanings to studies of the organizational work necessary to project those meanings, and of the interests and resources that function as incentives making the work worth doing and the meanings worth projecting and sustaining. Note, in this respect, how recent controversies over the Olympic Games and the Miss America contest reveal the vulnerability of their integrative functions to international politics, to the economic dimensions of "amateur" athletic competition, and to recently spawned ideological differences about the appropriate image of the ideal woman.

But in addition to the highly ceremonialized recurrent ritual practices, I also have in mind what is in a sense their opposite: the most informal kinds of habitual conversation (lore, gossip, "small talk") through which people convey their mostly unrehearsed feelings about the meanings of the routine matters that occupy everyday lives: love, sex, and friendship; marriage, family, houses, children, and schooling; food, drink, clothing, fashion, money, and health; sport, music, movies, television, and other leisure activities; and above all, how talk about these matters shapes our talk about the character and reputation of other people. Such topics are resonant with the common culture; they tap it, reproduce it, and in subtle ways reveal the changes it has undergone or is undergoing. But the *different* ways in which we talk about these topics reveal (among other things) the differences in the impact of social structure on how we "process" a culture presumably (even admittedly) shared but which can actually accommodate a wide variety of interpretive application to concrete circumstances.

For example: the differences in the ways in which we talk about romantic love (sentimentally, cynically, rationalistically, passionately) can reveal the ways in which differently situated persons cope with the consequences of the cultural injunction that we *must* fall in love. Let me speak carefully here. Does it seem odd to say that falling in love, perhaps the most "spontaneous" (and yet deliberately mystified) of our cultural practices, is something obligatory? It is surely no odder than Durkheim's efforts to find predictable pattern in suicide rates precisely *because* suicide was the most personal and private of acts. In our society, love is the only *fully* legitimate grounds for marriage (at least for first marriages, though increasingly for subsequent ones). There are of course other reasons for marrying (companionship, security, money, alliance— Foucault has written brilliantly on alliance and sexuality in the family), but none are as good as marrying for love. If, then, the establishment of new families through marriage is a strong social desideratum (if not, as functionalists used to say, a functional requisite), and if love is regarded as the most fully legitimate basis for marriage, then those of us who would be happily wed "must" fall in love—on pain of being denied the best that life has to offer. For a person older than, say, twenty-five, to confess to never having been in love is to be met with pity, a pity that humiliates rather than empathizes.

Though the culture is clear about the desirability of spousal love, it is not at all clear about how to cope with the elusiveness and instability of romantic love. The secret of how to sustain romantic love may be the only secret the world has ever kept. Should a cooled or routinized marriage be "worked at" rationally, perhaps with the aid of a counselor, aiming toward a mature and friendly companionship to replace the dampened fire of youthful sexual ardor? Should a cruise, an idyllic vacation on a Caribbean beach (without the children) be used to stir the embers and rekindle the flames? Or should the marriage be ended, to be replaced with new fire and a new partner? Or should extramarital fire be used to supplement domestic coziness? What we talk about (and how we talk about it) when we talk about romantic love, then, may be understood as ideological expressions of the differences in the resources provided by social placement for coping with a common cultural problem—much in the way that Robert Merton's well-known classifications of deviant modes of adaptation are behavioral expressions of the social fact that culture asks everyone to reach for success but that social structure provides different kinds of resources and opportunities for doing so.

In addition to public policy studies of culture and studies of society-wide celebratory ritual and informal talk, there should also be historical and ethnographic studies of the social stratification of culture, both in the major subgroups of complex industrial societies and in those institutional sectors (art, science, entertainment, advertising, journalism) primarily devoted to the production and distribution of symbolic culture—with their inextricable connections to technology, commerce, and industry. An historical time frame can provide perspective on unanticipated consequences almost impossible to obtain from one-shot survey data. The imperatives of elite "good taste," for example, may become dysfunctional for maintaining the conditions of its acquisition; a cultural aversion to business or commerce may disqualify one from seizing the opportunities they present to maintain the freedom from economic necessity implicit in high culture's claims to "purity." That is exactly what happened to at least some of the nineteenth-century British aristocracy. On the other hand, in several parts of the world some of the unanticipated consequences of modernist culture have generated a fierce "fundamentalist" reaction involving very odd alliances between elites and peasants or other ordinary folk.

As to fieldwork studies in contemporary settings, it seems likely that cultural struggles go on more or less continuously between and among the staffs, boards, and committees of galleries and museums, symphony and opera associations, theatrical companies, fashion houses, publishing firms, universities, foundations, and the great restaurants and cooking schools over exhibitions, purchases, performances, repertoires, publication lists, designs, curricula, cuisine, and grant policies. In addition, critics, editors, impresarios, curators, buyers, conductors, directors, chefs, and so on are more or less continually betting their cultural capital (and money) on the outcomes of their investment decisions in markets where they are pitted against opposing or competing kinds of investments. We do not have nearly enough participant-observer studies of such settings to give us a clear sense of the actual processes through which such struggles are conducted or of the firepower of the weapons being used. Robert Brustein's account in 1993 of the firing of JoAnne Akalaitis, artistic director of New York's Public Theater, provides only relatively prudent hints (from a theater insider) of the pressures placed on boards by influential critics, subscribers, and others.

Included here among studies of the social stratification of culture, of course, are the kinds of issues suggested by the debates over "brows," the relation of high culture to popular culture and to folk, ethnic, or youth cultures, and the role of mass media as "culture industries" that, by conceiving audiences almost exclusively as markets, either marginalize the culture of groups too small to interest advertisers of mass-produced products or relegate them to the nonprofit sector, which is dependent on the uncertain largesse of "responsible" corporations, wealthy private donors, or public subsidy (Schudson 1984; Schiller 1989; Gitlin 1983; DiMaggio 1986; Levine 1988; Becker 1982; Gans 1974; Jules-Rosette 1984; Hebdige 1979). Also included should be studies of milieux (villages, neighborhoods, occupations, deviant life-styles) and the adaptations by their cultural heritages to pressures put upon them by technological innovation, economic transformations, political conflict, and other crises or exigencies of circumstance (Mukerji 1989; Gans 1974; Whyte 1943; Stack 1974; Berger 1981; Liebow 1967; Anderson 1978).

It is, of course conceivable, even probable, that particular studies may straddle two or more of the focuses outlined here. Rock concerts (for anyone who has been to them) may be understood, for example, simultaneously as celebratory ritual (for youthfulness), an aggressive claim by a youth culture for greater public respect (viz. the benefit concerts in behalf of farmers, AIDS victims, South Africa, etc.), and as a particular form of industrial popular culture that may not fall unambiguously into any of the familiar "brow" categories. Of all the different dimensions of "youth culture" pop music is perhaps the most important, not simply because of its preoccupations with love, sex, identity, alienation, and other expressive dimensions of youth's actual dispositions and aversions, and not only because the music is sufficiently differentiated aesthetically to sustain different "brow" levels (these are "purely" cultural matters), but because performance of the music itself is the occasion for large and small gatherings of age-homogeneous groups and crowds, where young people may get some of their necessary and exploratory coupling-work done (not very different, structurally speaking, from the ways in which edifying lectures or sermons are, for church-related youth, the occasions for the cookies-and-punch sociability that follows them). Youth are, of course, also a major market for audio equipment and perhaps *the* major market for pop recordings, the latter being something that falls off sharply after marriage, and particularly after the couple begins to raise children—although after a divorce, stereos are among the first purchases by newly single people, and CD buying may pick up too—indications that singles are back into the coupling market.

Sociological analysis of the pop music dimensions of youth culture is also a good example of the sort of sociology of culture that few of the youthful fans of the music want to hear. The music is very much *their* music, and precious to them because of its association with several of the important experiences of growing up. Their tastes in the music usually get fixed in late adolescence and persist into adulthood. Earlier styles of the music are likely to be regarded as bland, quaint, irrelevant; subsequent styles as a perhaps pathological decline from a great period of the music's evolution. Unlike the repertoires of classical music, rock music is periodically (every four or five years) subjected to calls for new styles, new themes, new images, new breakthroughs, and this transient newness serves to identify the audience with prominent performers and its adulation of them. Because the music is so personally precious, any attempt to generalize about the structured and impersonal relation of the music to successive cohorts of its adolescent and postadolescent audiences seems much like a desecration, an expropriation.

A final set of studies may be designated as the social psychology of many of the matters touched on above. By "social psychology," here, I mean efforts to discover how the phenomena I have been calling culture, ideology, and interests (which thus far I have been conceiving primarily as "out there" structures, objectively describable or inferable) become part of the subjective identity of persons, experienced "in here" as beliefs, opinions, knowledge, tastes, preferences, and the emotions appropriate to the circumstances in which they are felt (e.g., grief at funerals, shame at disgrace). These issues have been a traditional part of the study of "socialization and internalization," which has a long and seldom enlightening literature (for some of the more helpful literature see Skinner 1971; Scott 1971; Berger and Luckmann 1966; Scheff 1990; Hochschild 1983; and Bourdieu 1977—especially on "habitus"). In recent years, the so-called cognitive turn in several social sciences concerned with the subjective processing of information has put the old questions in terms of what we need to know and need to feel in order to understand (or function adequately as a participant in) a society— and how we acquire what we need to know and feel. Such studies have emphasized the necessarily interpretive procedures involved in understanding everything from cultural rules to bureaucratic practices to the most tentative gesturing by strangers in the street (Cicourel 1974; Bailey 1983; Mehan 1975).

In a recent PBS report on Puerto Rican fighting gangs in New York, for example, one of the gang members described to the reporter a process he called "looking for a vic" (victim), which required an interpretation of gait, posture, and other body language that the gang member was able to describe in some detail. At another point in the taped report, the gang member hurriedly ushers the reporter to a safe place when rumors of an imminent gang fight are brought to him. Later, the reporter asks why he was so solicitous of her safety. He says that they like her *because* she shows no fear of them, but not simply because they imputed "courage" to her (which they valued highly) but because her lack of fear made *them* feel like basically ordinary people who were nevertheless interesting enough to be worth interviewing, rather than like an abstract fearsome (i.e., reified, dehumanized) "gang," the scourge of the streets of New York.

One of the things I have been trying to suggest in this section is that the conventional association of cultural studies with art, entertainment, fashion, advertising and such, rests on a common assumption that these forms are especially rich with symbolic meanings, which they draw from the common stock of extant culture, reproduce, add to, and alter. Although such studies are a central part of a program of research in the sociology of culture, it is worth remembering what was stressed earlier in this essay: that societies vary in how differentiated their institutions are, and the various kinds of differentiation are likely to affect the ways in which the richness of culture is distributed among its human carriers. There was a slogan, a survival from the 1960s I believe, permanently affixed to a courtyard wall at my daughter's high school that read, "We have no art; we do everything as well as we can"—which suggests, of course, that before "art" was differentiated as a special (and institutionalized) form of human activity, aesthetic meanings, like other meanings, were (and still are) implicit in and symbolically carried by all sort of social activity and its products.

This essay takes that fact into account by extending cultural studies beyond the differentiated realms of art, entertainment, sport, and so on to studies of milieux (or subcultures), of public ceremonies and informal talk that attempt to circumscribe or unify the differences of milieux, of public policy conflicts over issues that involve "deep" values recalcitrant to compromise or negotiation, and finally to *how* these general and specialized values (cognitive, aesthetic, moral) are communicated to younger generations and hence sustained (or not sustained) through historical time.

23 / CONCLUDING REMARKS

For some, the task of a sociology and social psychology of culture may seem too formidable. Surely, felt culture is very complex, and the linkages between specific settings, cultural obligation, ideological work, and their internalization into socially structured feeling are perennially elusive. But we are not without models and exemplars. Erving Goffman, for example, was expert in these matters. He describes the hand-holding of lovers: male *takes* female's hand; she allows her hand to be taken; the hands of the holder and the held occupy the same positions as those of a parent and child when crossing a busy street. The position of the male's hands is a "tie-sign" that conveys ("means") protection, care, dominance, and that affirms old gender and authority relations. As feminists are happy to show, those relations (and their correlated feelings) are weakened, even destroyed, when the positions of the hands are reversed. Take another example: a former convent student describes how the Church teaches its novice nuns not only to behave with humility but to *feel* humble. It requires each novice to take very small steps, with one shoulder brushing a wall, when walking through the corridors of the convent. Why this ritualized behavior produces immediate feelings of self-unimportance may be mysterious but not so mysterious as to defy sociological analysis. Surely social status has some connection to the amounts of cubic space one's body can confidently command (no purposeful striding down the center of the corridor), and the pace of one's stride (no "stridence"?) is a conventional measure of that command. A final example: in his short novel *Seize the Day*, Saul Bellow (trained, by the way, as an anthropologist) describes a middle-aged man who has had a very bad day. He is humiliated by his wealthy and aged father on whom he is still financially dependent; both his ex-wife and his present girlfriend rub his face in his inadequacies; his bank refuses a loan—a very bad day. At the end of the workday he wanders into the dense rush-hour streets of New York and is inadvertently jostled by the crowd into a funeral parlor where a service is taking place. There among the mourners viewing the body, he is permitted to release his grief. He is the only one to break down into uncontrolled sobbing, which evokes inference and comment from others present: he must be a member of the family to be so affected by the loss; the deceased must have been a wonderful person to have earned such authentic grief.

No one provides subtler or more complex descriptions of human culture than great novelists do. But the greatest of them cast those descriptions in a form or structure that renders the described events plausible, persuasive, probable, even inevitable. The logical structure says: given the setting and the relations generated among the characters within it, *the outcome is not likely to have been otherwise.* We should expect no less from a sociology of culture.

BIBLIOGRAPHY

Alexander, Jeffrey. 1987. *Twenty Lectures*. New York: Columbia University Press.

Alexander, Jeffrey, and Steven Seidman, eds. 1990. *Culture and Society*. New York: Cambridge University Press.

Althusser, Louis. 1972. *Leninism and Other Essays*. New York: Monthly Review Press.

Anderson, Elijah. 1978. *A Place on the Corner*. Chicago: University of Chicago Press.

Ariès, Phillippe. 1962. *Centuries of Childhood*. New York: Knopf.

Arnold, Matthew. [1869] 1971. *Culture and Anarchy*. Indianapolis: Bobbs-Merrill.

Bailey, Frederick. 1983. *The Tactical Uses of Passion*. Ithaca, N.Y.: Cornell University Press.

Barnes, J. A. 1994. *A Pack of Lies: Toward a Sociology of Lying*. Cambridge: Cambridge University Press.

Becker, Howard S. *Outsiders*. 1963. London: Free Press of Glencoe.

———. 1982. *Art Worlds*. Berkeley: University of California Press.

———, ed. 1964. *The Other Side*. New York: Free Press.

Bell, Daniel. 1976. *The Cultural Contradictions of Capitalism*. New York: Basic Books.

Bellah, Robert, Richard Madsen, William M. Sullivan, Ann Swidler, Steven M. Tipton. 1985. *Habits of the Heart*. Berkeley: University of California Press.

Bellow, Saul. 1956. *Seize the Day*. New York: Viking Press.

Benedict, Ruth. 1946. *Patterns of Culture*. New York: Penguin Books.

Berger, Bennett M. 1971. "Sociology and the Intellectuals." In *Looking for America*. Englewood Cliffs, N.J.: Prentice-Hall.

———. 1981. *The Survival of a Counterculture*. Berkeley: University of California Press.

———. 1986. "Taste and Domination." *American Journal of Sociology* 91, no. 6: 1445–53.

———, ed. 1990. *Authors of Their Own Lives*. Berkeley: University of California Press.

Berger, Peter L., and Thomas Luckmann. 1966. *The Social Construction of Reality*. Garden City, N.Y.: Doubleday.

Bernstein, Basil. 1975. *Class, Codes, and Control*. New York: Schocken Books.

Bloor, David. 1991. *Knowledge and Social Imagery*. Chicago: University of Chicago Press.

Boas, Franz. 1938. *General Anthropology*. Boston: Heath.

Boltanski, Luc, and Laurent Thevenot. 1991. *De la justification*. Paris: Gallimard.

Boudon, Raymond. 1986. *L'ideologie*. Paris: Fayard.

Bourdieu, Pierre. 1977. *Outline of a Theory of Practice*. New York: Cambridge University Press.

———. 1984. *Distinction*. Cambridge: Harvard University Press.

———. 1988. *Homo Academicus*. Cambridge: Polity Press.

Bourdieu, Pierre, and Jean-Claude Passeron. 1977. *Reproduction in Education, Society, and Culture*. Beverly Hills, Calif.: Sage Publications.

Bourdieu, Pierre, and Löic J. D. Wacquant. 1992. *An Invitation to Reflexive Sociology*. Chicago: University of Chicago Press.

Bowles, Samuel, and Herbert Gintis. 1976. *Schooling in Capitalist America*. New York: Basic Books.

Boyd, Robert, and Peter J. Richerson. 1985. *Culture and the Evolutionary Process*. Chicago: University of Chicago Press.

Brooks, Van Wyck. 1958. *From a Writer's Notebook*. New York: Dutton.

Cicourel, Aaron. 1974. *Cognitive Sociology*. New York: Free Press.

Clifford, James, and George Marcus. 1986. *Writing Culture*. Berkeley: University of California Press.

Cohen, Albert. 1955. *Delinquent Boys*. Glencoe, Ill.: Free Press.

Collins, Randall. 1981. *Sociology since Midcentury*. New York: Academic Press.

Collins, Richard, James Curran, Nicholas Garnham, Paddy Scannell, Philip Schlesinger, and Colin Sparks, eds. 1986. *Media, Culture and Society*. Beverly Hills, Calif.: Sage Publications.

Conrad, Joseph. 1923. *Lord Jim*. London: J. M. Dent.

Coser, Lewis. 1974. *Greedy Institutions*. New York: Free Press.

Coser, Rose Laub. 1991. *In Defense of Modernity*. Stanford: Stanford University Press.

Cowley, Malcolm. 1958. *The Literary Situation*. New York: Viking Press.

Davis, Susan. 1986. *Parades and Power*. Philadelphia: Temple University Press.

Dimaggio, Paul. 1986a. "Cultural Entrepreneurship in Nineteenth-Century Boston." In *Media, Culture and Society*, edited by Richard Collins et al. Beverly Hills, Calif.: Sage Publications.

———. 1988. *Managers of the Arts*. Washington, D.C.: Seven Locks Press.

———, ed. 1986b. *Non-Profit Enterprises in the Arts*. New York: Oxford University Press.

Disraeli, Benjamin. 1956. *Sybil, or the Two Nations*. London: Oxford University Press.

Douglas, Ann. 1977. *The Feminization of American Culture*. New York: Knopf.

Douglas, Jack D. 1967. *The Social Meanings of Suicide*. Princeton: Princeton University Press.

Douglas, Mary. 1969. *Purity and Danger*. New York: Praeger.

———. 1986. *How Institutions Think*. Syracuse: Syracuse University Press.

Douglas, Mary, and Baron Isherwood. 1979. *The World of Goods*. New York: Basic Books.

Elias, Norbert. 1983. *The Court Society*. New York: Pantheon Books.

Eliot, T. S. 1921. *The Sacred Wood*. New York: Knopf.

———. 1949. *Notes toward the Definition of Culture*. New York: Harcourt, Brace.

Feyerabend, Paul K. 1988. *Against Method*. Revised edition. London: Verso.

Fiedler, Leslie. 1955. *An End to Innocence*. Boston: Beacon Press.

———. 1971. *The Collected Essays of Leslie Fiedler*. New York: Stein and Day.

Foley, Douglas. 1990. *Learning Capitalist Culture*. Philadelphia: University of Pennsylvania Press.

Foucault, Michel. 1965. *Madness and Civilization*. London: Tavistock Publications.

———. 1978. *The History of Sexuality*. New York: Pantheon Books.

————. 1980. *Power/Knowledge.* New York: Pantheon Books.

Fromm, Erich. 1941. *Escape from Freedom.* New York: Rinehart and Winston.

Gaines, Donna. 1991. *Teenage Wasteland.* New York: Pantheon Books.

Galbraith, J. K. [Mark Epernay, pseud.]. 1963. *The McLandress Dimension.* Boston: Houghton Mifflin.

————. 1969. *The Affluent Society.* Boston: Houghton Mifflin.

Gans, Herbert. 1974. *Popular Culture and High Culture.* New York: Basic Books.

Garfinkel, Harold. 1967. *Studies in Ethnomethodology.* Englewood Cliffs, N.J.: Prentice-Hall.

Geertz, Clifford. 1973. *The Interpretation of Cultures.* New York: Basic Books.

————. 1983. *Local Knowledge.* New York: Basic Books.

————. 1988. *Works and Lives.* Stanford: Stanford University Press.

Gerth, Hans, and C. Wright Mills. 1953. *Character and Social Structure.* New York: Harcourt, Brace.

Giroux, Henry, 1981. *Ideology, Culture, and the Process of Schooling.* Philadelphia: Temple University Press.

Gitlin, Todd. 1983. *Inside Prime Time.* New York: Pantheon Books.

————. 1987. *The Sixties.* New York: Bantam Books.

Glazer, Nathan. 1990. "From Socialism to Sociology." In *Authors of Their Own Lives,* edited by Bennett M. Berger. Berkeley: University of California Press.

Goffman, Erving. 1971. *Relations in Public.* New York: Basic Books.

Gouldner, Alvin W. 1970. *The Coming Crisis of American Sociology.* New York: Basic Books.

————. 1974. *The Dark Side of the Dialectic.* Dublin: Economic and Social Research Institute.

————. 1976. *The Dialectic of Ideology and Technology.* New York: Seabury Press.

Gramsci, Antonio. 1971. *Selections from the Prison Notebooks.* London: Lawrence and Wishart.

Greeley, Andrew M. 1990. "The Crooked Lines of God." In *Authors of Their Own Lives,* edited by Bennett M. Berger. Berkeley: University of California Press.

Greimas, A. J. 1982. *Semiotics and Language.* Indianapolis: Indiana University Press.

Gross, Paul R., and Norman Levitt. 1994. *Higher Superstition.* Baltimore: Johns Hopkins University Press.

Gusfield, Joseph. 1962. *Symbolic Crusade.* Urbana: University of Illinois Press.

Gutman, Herbert G. 1976. *The Black Family in Slavery and Freedom.* New York: Pantheon Books.

———. 1987. *Power and Culture.* New York: Pantheon Books.

Hallin, Daniel. 1986. *The Uncensored War.* New York: Oxford University Press.

Hawthorn, Geoffrey. 1990. "The Fall of Economic Man." *The New Republic,* February 5, pp. 34–38.

Hebdige, Dick. 1979. *Subculture.* London: Methuen.

Herder, J. G. 1969. *J. G. Herder on Social and Political Culture.* London: Cambridge University Press.

Hirschman, Albert. 1977. *The Passions and the Interests.* Princeton: Princeton University Press.

Hobsbawm, E. J. 1964. *Laboring Men.* New York: Basic Books.

Hochschild, Arlie. 1983. *The Managed Heart.* Berkeley: University of California Press.

Hoggart, Richard. 1967. *The Uses of Literacy.* London: Chatto and Windus.

Hulme, Kathryn. 1956. *The Nun's Story.* Boston: Little, Brown.

Jackson, Robert. 1988. *An Irresistible Force.* New York: Cambridge University Press.

Jacoby, Russell. 1987. *The Last Intellectuals.* New York: Basic Books.

Jaeger, Gertrude, and Philip Selznick. 1964. "A Normative Theory of Culture." *American Sociological Review* 24, no. 5, pp. 653–69.

Johnson, Leslie. 1979. *The Culture Critics.* London: Routledge and Kegan Paul.

Jules-Rosette, Bennetta. 1984. *The Messages of Tourist Art.* New York: Plenum Press.

Kael, Pauline. 1994. "Reflections" and "Interview." *The New Yorker,* March 21.

Kahn, Herman. 1966. *Thinking about the Unthinkable.* New York: Avon Books.

Kanter, Rosabeth. 1972. *Commitment and Community.* Cambridge: Harvard University Press.

Katz, Jack. 1988. *Seductions of Crime.* New York: Basic Books.

Kroeber, Alfred, ed. 1953. *Anthropology Today.* Chicago: University of Chicago Press.

Kroeber, Alfred, and Clyde Kluckhohn. 1952. *Culture.* New York: Random House.

Kuhn, Thomas. 1962. *The Structure of Scientific Revolutions.* Chicago: University of Chicago Press.

Ladurie, Emanuel Le Roy. 1974. *The Peasants of Languedoc.* Urbana: University of Illinois Press.

———. 1979. *Carnival in Romans.* New York: George Braziller.

Lamont, Michele. 1992. *Money, Morals, and Manners.* Chicago: University of Chicago Press.

Latour, Bruno. 1989. *The Pasteurization of France.* Cambridge: Harvard University Press.

Latour, Bruno, and Steve Woolgar. 1979. *Laboratory Life.* Beverly Hills, Calif.: Sage Publications.

Lemert, Edwin. 1967. *Human Deviance, Social Problems, and Social Control.* Englewood Cliffs, N.J.: Prentice-Hall.

Levine, Lawrence. 1988. *Highbrow/Lowbrow.* Cambridge: Harvard University Press.

Lévi-Strauss, Claude. 1966. *The Savage Mind.* Chicago: University of Chicago Press.

———. 1969. *The Elementary Structures of Kinship.* Boston: Beacon Press.

Liebow, Elliott. 1967. *Talley's Corner.* Boston: Little, Brown.

Lipsitz, George. 1990. *Time Passages.* Minneapolis: University of Minnesota Press.

Lowenthal, Leo. 1956. *Literature and the Image of Man.* Boston: Beacon Press.

———. 1984. *Literature and Mass Culture.* New Brunswick, N.J.: Transaction Books.

Luker, Kristin. 1975. *Taking Chances.* Berkeley: University of California Press.

———. 1984. *Abortion and the Politics of Motherhood.* Berkeley: University of California Press.

Lynes, Russell. 1957. *A Surfeit of Honey.* New York: Harper and Co.

———. 1966. *Confessions of a Dilettante.* New York: Harper and Row.

Macaloon, John. 1981. *This Great Symbol.* Chicago: University of Chicago Press.

———, ed. 1984. *Rite, Drama, Festival, Spectacle.* Philadelphia: Institute for the Study of Human Issues.

MacDonald, Dwight. 1965. *Masscult and Midcult.* New York: Partisan Review.

MacIver, Robert. 1937. *Society.* New York: Farrar and Rinehart.

Mailer, Norman. 1957. "The White Negro." *Dissent* 4, no. 3, pp. 276–93.

Mannheim, Karl. 1936. *Ideology and Utopia.* New York: Harcourt, Brace.

Mead, Margaret. 1978. *Culture and Commitment*. New York: Columbia University Press.

Mehan, Hugh. 1975. *The Reality of Ethnomethodology*. New York: John Wiley.

Mills, C. Wright. 1951. *White Collar*. New York: Oxford University Press.

Merton, Robert K. 1957. *Social Theory and Social Structure*. Glencoe, Ill.: Free Press.

Merton, Robert K., and Robert A. Nisbet, eds. 1961. *Contemporary Social Problems*. New York: Harcourt Brace Jovanovich.

Mukerji, Chandra. 1989. *A Fragile Power*. Princeton: Princeton University Press.

Nabokov, Vladimir. 1981. *Lectures on Literature*. New York: Harcourt Brace Jovanovich.

Nisbet, Robert A. 1953. *The Quest for Community*. New York: Oxford University Press.

———. 1966. *The Sociological Tradition*. New York: Basic Books.

Orwell, George. 1981. *1984*. New York: New American Library.

Parsons, Talcott. 1949. *The Structure of Social Action*. Glencoe, Ill.: Free Press.

———. 1951. *The Social System*. New York: Free Press.

Phillips, David. 1988. Unpublished manuscript on Miss America. University of California, San Diego.

Polanyi, Karl. 1958. *Personal Knowledge*. Chicago: University of Chicago Press.

Real, Michael. 1977. *Mass-Mediated Culture*. Englewood Cliffs, N.J.: Prentice-Hall.

Riesman, David. 1950. *The Lonely Crowd*. New Haven: Yale University Press.

Rorty, Richard. 1989. *Contingency, Irony, and Solidarity*. New York: Cambridge University Press.

Sahlins, Marshall. 1976. *Culture and Practical Reason*. Chicago: University of Chicago Press.

Said, Edward. 1978. *Orientalism*. New York: Pantheon Books.

———. 1993. *Culture and Imperialism*. New York: Knopf.

Scheff, Thomas. 1990. *Microsociology: Discourse, Emotion, and Social Structure*. Chicago: University of Chicago Press.

Schiller, Herbert. 1989. *Culture, Inc*. New York: Oxford University Press.

Schneider, Mark. 1993. *Culture and Enchantment*. Chicago: University of Chicago Press.

Schudson, Michael. 1984. *Advertising, the Uneasy Persuasion*. New York: Basic Books.

——. 1989. "How Culture Works." *Theory and Society* 18, no. 2, pp. 153–80.

Scott, John Finley. 1971. *Internalization of Norms*. Englewood Cliffs, N.J.: Prentice-Hall.

Scull, Andrew. 1979. *Museums of Madness*. New York: St. Martin's Press.

Shils, Edward. 1957. "Daydreams and Nightmares: Reflections on the Criticism of Mass Culture." *Sewanee Review* 65, no. 4, pp. 587–608.

Shilts, Randy. 1987. *And the Band Played On*. New York: St. Martin's Press.

Simmel, Georg. 1950. *The Sociology of Georg Simmel*. Glencoe, Ill.: Free Press.

——. 1955. *Conflict and the Web of Group Affiliations*. New York: Free Press.

——. 1971. *On Individuality and Social Forms*. Chicago: University of Chicago Press.

Skinner, B. F. 1971. *Beyond Freedom and Dignity*. New York: Knopf.

Slater, Philip. 1966. *Microcosm*. New York: John Wiley.

Spiro, Melford. 1987. *Culture and Human Nature*. Chicago: University of Chicago Press.

Spitzer, Leo. 1942. "*Milieu* and *Ambiance*." *Philosophy and Phenomenological Research* 3, pp. 1–42; 169–218.

Stack, Carol B. 1974. *All Our Kin*. New York: Harper and Row.

Stendhal [Marie-Henri Beyle]. 1953. *The Red and the Black*. New York: Modern Library.

Stouffer, Samuel. 1955. *Communism, Conformity, and Civil Liberties*. Garden City, N.Y.: Doubleday.

Sumner, W. G. 1960. *Folkways*. New York: New American Library.

Sutherland, Edwin. 1956. *The Sutherland Papers*. Bloomimgton: Indiana University Press.

——. 1961. *White Collar Crime*. New York: Holt, Rinehart, and Winston.

Swidler, Ann. 1986. "Culture in Action." *American Sociological Review* 51, no. 2, pp. 273–86.

——. n. d. Talk of Love. Unpublished manuscript.

Thompson, E. P. 1964. *The Making of the English Working Class*. New York: Pantheon Books.

Thompson, Michael, Richard Ellis, and Aaron Wildavsky. 1990. *Cultural Theory*. Boulder, Colo.: Westview Press.

Trilling, Lionel. 1951. *Freud and the Crisis of Our Culture*. Boston: Beacon Press.

———. 1979. *Of This Time, of That Place, and Other Stories*. New York: Harcourt Brace Jovanovich.

Tylor, Edward. 1958. *Primitive Culture*. New York: Harper and Co.

Van Maanen, John. 1988. *Tales of the Field*. Chicago: University of Chicago Press.

Warner, Sam. 1962. *Streetcar Suburbs*. Cambridge: Harvard University Press.

Weber, Max. 1956. *From Max Weber, Essays in Sociology*. New York: Oxford University Press.

———. 1958. *The Protestant Ethic and the Spirit of Capitalism*. New York: Scribner's.

Wellek, René, and Austin Warren. 1955. *Theory of Literature*. London: Jonathan Cape.

Whyte, W. F. 1943. *Street Corner Society*. Chicago: University of Chicago Press.

Williams, Raymond. 1976. *Keywords*. New York: Oxford University Press.

———. 1981. *Culture*. London: Fontana.

Willis, Paul. 1981. *Learning to Labor*. New York: Columbia University Press.

Wilson, Edmund. 1941. *The Wound and the Bow*. New York: Oxford University Press.

Wolff, Janet. Forthcoming. *Resident Alien*. New Haven: Yale University Press.

Wright, Will. 1975. *Sixguns and Society*. Berkeley: University of California Press.

Wrong, Dennis. 1961. "The Oversocialized Conception of Man in Modern Sociology." *American Sociological Review* 26, no. 2, pp. 183–93.

Wuthnow, Robert, James Davison Hunter, Albert Bergesen, and Edith Kurzweil. 1984. *Cultural Analysis*. Boston: Routledge and Kegan Paul.

INDEX

Compositor:	Graphic Composition, Inc.
Text:	10/15 Janson
Display:	Janson
Printer:	BookCrafters
Binder:	BookCrafters